SOUL KEEPING

Resources by John Ortberg

Everybody's Normal Till You Get to Know Them
(book, ebook, audio)

God Is Closer Than You Think
(book, ebook, audio, curriculum with Stephen and Amanda Sorenson)

*If You Want to Walk on Water,
You've Got to Get Out of the Boat*
(book, ebook, audio, curriculum with Stephen and Amanda Sorenson)

Know Doubt
(book, ebook, previously titled *Faith and Doubt*)

The Life You've Always Wanted
(book, ebook, audio, curriculum with Stephen and Amanda Sorenson)

Love Beyond Reason

The Me I Want to Be
(book, ebook, audio, curriculum with Scott Rubin)

Soul Keeping
(book, ebook, curriculum with Christine M. Anderson)

When the Game Is Over, It All Goes Back in the Box
(book, ebook, audio, curriculum with Stephen and Amanda Sorenson)

Who Is This Man?
(book, ebook, audio, curriculum with Christine M. Anderson)

SOUL KEEPING

CARING *for* THE MOST IMPORTANT
PART *of* YOU

JOHN ORTBERG

ZONDERVAN

Soul Keeping
Copyright © 2014 by John Ortberg

This title is also available as a Zondervan ebook.
Visit www.zondervan.com/ebooks.

Requests for information should be addressed to:
Zondervan, 3900 Sparks Dr. SE, Grand Rapids, Michigan 49546

ISBN 978-0-310-27597-8

International Trade Paper Edition

Cover design: Curt Diepenhorst
Cover and interior photography: Tolga Sipahi / Getty Images®
Interior design: Beth Shagene

Printed in the United States of America

To Dallas Albert Willard
(1935–2013)

*An unceasing spiritual being with an eternal destiny
in God's great universe.*

"In those days there were giants in the land ..."

CONTENTS

CONTENTS

FOREWORD

BY DR. HENRY CLOUD

As John Ortberg talks about the "soul," I remember a moment as if it were yesterday. I was a clinical director of a Christian psychiatric hospital, and we were having the weekly meeting that we called "Staffing." It was the time, each Wednesday, when the doctors, psychologists nurses, therapists, art and music therapists, and group therapists all got together to go over each patient's treatment. We would talk about what was happening with them in the groups and in their individual therapy, their progress, and our action plans to help.

I loved this time each week. It was a rich time of seeing a group of dedicated professionals come together to truly care for, discuss, and plan goodness for the people they were trying to help. We celebrated patient's successes, breakthroughs, and the like, and we agonized over their difficulties and misfortunes. It was one of the best examples of community love that I have ever seen ... people bringing their gifts together in the service of others.

"Sarah did it! Last night in family group she finally told her mother that she was not going to take the job Mom has been pressuring her to take, and was going to figure out her own path. It was awesome," a nurse reported. We all cheered as we experienced the fruitfulness of Sarah's hard work.

"Alex is having a hard time this week ... he found out that his uncle who has held him together is moving, and he is afraid of what he is going to do without him. He fears going back to drugs and his old friends," his therapist reported.

"Susan is gearing up for discharge. She has done great ... ready to go back to grad school now, energy has returned, and she is stable. I think everything is in place ... depression is gone, and she hasn't binged and purged at all," said Susan's psychologist. We were all so happy for her.

Then came the moment I will always remember.

It was time to talk about Maddie, and I could tell everyone's expression changed. "Fell" would be a better word. Why? Maddie was a very difficult person to like. She had developed a way about her that was off-putting, even when she was seemingly engaged with others. It seemed that something was always wrong with others, with the world around her, even with us who were trying to help her. Her husband was all too familiar with being the one who was "wrong" as well.

We all turned to Graham, her psychologist, and I asked him what was happening with Maddie. That is when he made this statement:

"Well ... it seems that Maddie still has no interest in having an interior life."

I will never forget it. That statement said it all: Maddie had no interest in looking at her internal world. Her attitudes, her hurts, her strengths, her patterns of thinking and behaving, or not trusting and not risking, her spiritual life, and maybe most of all, her avoidance of embracing her real suffering and the courage to resolve it.

As a result, we all shared the same lack of hope for her, at least at this juncture. As long as she was not going to embrace her "interior life," we all knew that her "life" was not going to change much at all. Whereas with the other people our task was to help provide paths, skills, and resources for them to embrace and develop their interior and interpersonal world, with Maddie our task was to get her to see that she has one. There really is a "life" inside of her that gives rise to the external life she complains about every day.

That was our task ... to get Maddie to see, embrace, and develop her internal life—her *real* life.

John Ortberg is doing that for us in this book. I could not stop reflecting upon that day in the hospital as I read these pages. Graham's words, "Maddie has no interest in having an interior life," were words that can too often be applied to me, to others whom I work with, and to pretty much everyone I know ... at least at various moments. While we might not have a "clinical" problem such as depression or bulimia, we all have issues in life that emanate from our souls, from parts of the soul that have been ignored. It is the human condition; we ignore our internal life, and as a result, we do not have the outside "life" that we desire, relationally or functionally. We get lost, and we need help to be reminded to work on that internal "life," the real one ... what John is calling our "soul."

He reminds us that we have one and, as Jesus told us, that our soul is our real life. It is the one from which everything else emanates. It is the one that God breathed into mankind, when we became "living souls."

But John goes much farther than reminding us that we have a soul. He also becomes a loving "staff meeting" for all of us. He not only tells the Maddie in me that I need to take an interest in developing this interior life, but also gives me some real help in outlining some areas to focus on in the journey. In this book he becomes what John is at his best ... a spiritual guide.

This book will not only help you to realize that you have a soul, an interior life, and reveal its importance, but will also give you some tools and handles to grab as you develop that life. It will help you to get grounded again, or even for the first time, with the One who first breathed that life into you, and Who desires every day to breathe more and more life into every corner of your being. And it will remind you that your soul, your interior life that results in what happens on the outside, is not a temporary state. It is not a focus for your "quiet time" or just your spiritual journey ... a religious sector for the time being. As Jesus said, it is your *real* life, and you do not want to lose it. Now, or in the eternal future.

John reminds us that while we might be living in a body, or in a context of a career or family or community or service, there is a soul that integrates our whole person — will, mind, and body — into an "unceasing spiritual being with an eternal destiny in God's great universe." It is the ultimate reality of who you are, past today's circumstance or context. It is the eternal now that will be your eternal you. And that becomes a wake-up call and a motivator to do what the Maddie in me sometimes does not want to do: … take an interest in this internal life … take a diligent interest and stewardship of this life that God has breathed … this soul.

As I read, I was thankful to John for giving us this reminder and this guide. I don't know about you, but I need for someone from time to time to wake up the "Maddie in me" and remind me to make sure that I am doing what the Creator of this life tells me to do so that the life he gave me will continue into more and more life. And I need a guide to give me some steps. John has done both … awakened us and guided us.

So, take an interest in your internal life, and John will give you some very helpful guidance.

THE KEEPER
OF THE STREAM

There once was a town high in the Alps that straddled the banks of a beautiful stream. The stream was fed by springs that were old as the earth and deep as the sea.

The water was clear like crystal. Children laughed and played beside it; swans and geese swam on it. You could see the rocks and the sand and the rainbow trout that swarmed at the bottom of the stream.

High in the hills, far beyond anyone's sight, lived an old man who served as Keeper of the Springs. He had been hired so long ago that now no one could remember a time when he wasn't there. He would travel from one spring to another in the hills, removing branches or fallen leaves or debris that might pollute the water. But his work was unseen.

One year the town council decided they had better things to do with their money. No one supervised the old man anyway. They had roads to repair and taxes to collect and services to offer, and giving money to an unseen stream-cleaner had become a luxury they could no longer afford.

So the old man left his post. High in the mountains, the springs went untended; twigs and branches and worse muddied the liquid flow. Mud and silt compacted the creek bed; farm wastes turned parts of the stream into stagnant bogs.

For a time no one in the village noticed. But after a while, the water was not the same. It began to look brackish. The swans flew away to live elsewhere. The water no longer had a crisp scent that drew children to play by it. Some people in the town began to grow ill. All noticed the loss of sparkling beauty that used to flow between the banks of the streams that fed the town. The life of the village depended on the stream, and the life of the stream depended on the keeper.

The city council reconvened, the money was found, the old man was rehired. After yet another time, the springs were cleaned, the stream was pure, children played again on its banks, illness was replaced by health, the swans came home, and the village came back to life.

The life of a village depended on the health of the stream.

The stream is your soul. And you are the keeper.

Our soul is like a stream of water, which gives strength, direction, and harmony to every other area of our life. When that stream is as it should be, we are constantly refreshed and exuberant in all we do, because our soul itself is then profusely rooted in the vastness of God and his kingdom, including nature; and all else within us is enlivened and directed by that stream. Therefore we are in harmony with God, reality, and the rest of human nature and nature at large.

—DALLAS WILLARD
IN *RENOVATION OF THE HEART*

HOLY GROUND

Sometimes the soul gets sifted and shaped in places you could never imagine and ways you could never expect. For me it was in Box Canyon.

Box Canyon is a rocky hideaway tucked between Simi Valley and the San Fernando Valley west of Los Angeles. Cowboy B-movies and television westerns like *The Lone Ranger* used to be shot there. It is a hodgepodge of homes ranging from a castle built by a postal worker in the 1940s, to a converted water tower, to a two-story plywood home built over an outhouse. Its occupants tend not to take kindly to zoning officials, who have been known to be shot at and had their tires slashed. It has dirt roads leading to homes guarded by "No Trespassing" signs, or a local variant: "This property protected by shotgun law." Ten-thousand-square-foot mansions stand next door to cabins with rusting cars and farm machinery in their front yards. It is home to hippies and rednecks and nonconformists, with the occasional drug dealer thrown in for good measure. In 1948, a San Francisco divorcé calling himself Krishna Venta began a commune called WKFL (Wisdom, Knowledge, Faith, and Love), with this sign: "Ye who enter here enter upon holy ground." He said he was 244,000 years old and claimed to be Jesus Christ, but he died along with nine other members when two husbands jealous of his attentions to their wives tossed a bomb into WKFL.

Box Canyon has had two more-or-less-famous residents: one a cult leader and mass murderer named Charles Manson, and the other a writer and intellectual named Dallas Willard. Such are the possibilities of the human soul. Dallas was a retired professor of philosophy at the University of Southern California (USC). I first drove to his home on a sweltering August afternoon more than two decades ago. I had read a book by Dallas that moved me more than anything I had ever read. I was a young pastor at a small church in Simi Valley, California, and was surprised to learn that Dallas lived just a few miles away. I wrote to tell him how much his book meant to me, and to my surprise he wrote back inviting me to come visit him.

I suppose the truth is that a big part of why I went to see him is that he was (in my small world) a celebrity and that I thought if I could be around someone important, perhaps a little importance could rub off on me too. And maybe he could help me become more successful.

I did not know then what I would learn over many years — that he was a healer of souls. I did not know that his home in that quirky little canyon was a kind of spiritual hospital. Long ago, people used to speak of spiritual leaders as those who have been entrusted with the "cure of souls"; we get old words like *curate* from that expression. Dallas was the first soul curate I knew, although that's not a title bestowed by USC. I thought I might learn something about the soul from Dallas, but I did not know how hungry and thirsty my own soul was. I only knew that at moments when Dallas would look off into the distance as if he were seeing something I could not see and would speak about how good God is, I would find myself beginning to cry.

But before that first visit, all I knew of Dallas was that he taught philosophy at the University of Southern California and wrote about subjects such as spiritual disciplines. I pictured an East Coast, pipe-smoking, sherry-drinking Episcopalian who wore tweed jackets with elbow patches.

Not so much.

I found his address: a small house behind a white picket fence.

When he bought it fifty years ago, it overlooked a lake that has
long since dried up; now it offers an excellent view of the San
Fernando Valley smog.

Inside, furniture was scarce, old, and inexpensive. The house,
like Dallas's head, was mostly furnished with books. There was an
air conditioning unit in the living room window that was installed
forty years ago and roared like a jet engine, so you had to yell to
speak over it when it ran, which was not often. To say that Dallas
and his wife, Jane, were not materialistic would be like saying that
the pope doesn't date much. Dallas told me once about a construction worker he used to meet with to talk about soul matters. (The
picture of a scruffy concrete worker having long talks about God
and the soul with an erudite philosopher is a poignant one.) The
first time he saw Dallas's house, he went home and told his wife,
"Honey, I finally met someone with furniture worse than us." I
think Dallas took it as a compliment.

I was nervous when I knocked on the door, but Dallas was a
difficult person to remain nervous around. "Hello, Brother John,"
he said, and somehow I felt immediately accepted into a little circle
of belonging. He invited me in and offered me a glass of iced tea,
then sat down on his favorite chair across from an old sofa.

Dallas was larger than I had pictured, because I had not known
that he had played forward on his college basketball team. His hair
was wavy and steel-gray; he wore glasses; his clothes suggested that
he had long ago mastered Jesus' suggestion: "Do not worry about
what you should wear." When Dallas met his future wife, Jane, in a
small religious school called Tennessee Temple, she noticed he did
not wear socks and assumed it was because he was a rebel; she did
not know it was actually because he couldn't afford them.

His appearance was unremarkable except for two things. His
voice had the faint suggestion of British precision that all philoso-
phers seem to pick up, but it also carried the touch of the Missouri
hills. On the thinker/feeler scale, Dallas was almost pure thinker,
but there were times when in speaking or praying, his voice had a
tremulous note that suggested a heart that was nearly bursting over
some unseen wonder.

The other remarkable characteristic of his body was how unhurried it was. Someone said of him once, "I'd like to live in his time zone." I suppose if the house was on fire, he would have moved quickly to get out of it, but his face and the movements of his body all seemed to say that he had no place else to go and nothing in particular to worry about.

Many years later I had moved to Chicago. Entering into a very busy season of ministry, I called Dallas to ask him what I needed to do to stay spiritually healthy. I pictured him sitting in that room as we talked. There was a long pause — with Dallas there was nearly always a long pause — and then he said slowly, "You must ruthlessly eliminate hurry from your life." I quickly wrote that down. Most people take notes with Dallas; I have even seen his wife take notes, which my wife rarely does with me.

"Okay, Dallas," I responded. "I've got that one. Now what other spiritual nuggets do you have for me? I don't have a lot of time, and I want to get all the spiritual wisdom from you that I can."

"There is nothing else," he said, generously acting as if he did not notice my impatience. "Hurry is the great enemy of spiritual life in our day. You must ruthlessly eliminate hurry from your life."

> Hurry is the great enemy of spiritual life in our day. You must ruthlessly eliminate hurry from your life.
> DALLAS WILLARD

As I sipped my iced tea at that first meeting, Dallas asked me about my family and my work. The phone rang — this was before cell phones and answering machines — and he did not answer it. He didn't even look as if he wanted to answer it. He just went on talking with me as if there were no phone ringing, as if he actually wanted to talk with me more than to answer the telephone, even though it might be someone important. I had the odd sensation (I have talked to many others since then who have noticed the same thing) of having my own heart rate begin to slow down to match his.

The house fit him. Dallas grew up in the Great Depression in a part of rural Missouri that did not have electricity until he was eighteen years old. When he was age two, his mother died. Her final words to her husband were, "Keep eternity before the children." As a two-year-old boy, Dallas tried to climb inside the casket to be next to his mother's body. Since there was not enough money to keep the family together, Dallas was passed from one relative to another until he graduated from high school. Despite these circumstances, he was president of his senior class—all eleven members.

I began by asking him the questions that I thought were why I had come: How is it that people change; what makes change so hard; what does it mean exactly to say that human beings have souls, and why do souls matter? Why is it that I lead a church full of people who believe the right things about God and even read the Bible and pray, but don't seem to actually change much? Why don't I seem to change much?

He began to talk, and as he spoke, I couldn't help but think that he was the smartest man I had ever met. Many years later, when he was very sick, Nancy and I would spend a day packing up some of his books in a garage near his home. His primary library was in that home; his secondary library was in another home next door that he and Jane bought many years ago to catch the overflow; his tertiary library was at USC. We packed up more than one hundred boxes of books from his quaternary library, in that garage: books in Latin and German and Greek; books from the world's greatest minds and from backwoods country preachers. I tease sometimes that I never got in an argument with Dallas because I was afraid he would prove I don't exist.

Yet Dallas never made me feel stupid. I was dimly aware, as I talked to him, how badly I wanted to impress him with how smart I was, and how I couldn't turn that little "impress him" switch off in my mind even if I wanted to. Somebody said that if you're the smartest person in the room, you're in the wrong room.

Nevertheless, something about Dallas was so safe that I found myself offering unsolicited confessions. "I can't even talk without trying to sound impressive." I wanted to impress him, yet at the same time, I was ashamed of that wanting and knew life would be better without it, and that somehow this was a smart guy whose identity was not in his IQ.

Toward the end of one of his philosophy classes a student raised an objection that was both insulting toward Dallas and clearly wrong. Instead of correcting him, Dallas gently said that this would be a good place to end the class for the day. Afterward, a friend approached Dallas: "Why did you let him get away with that? Why didn't you demolish him?" Dallas replied, "I was practicing the discipline of not having to have the last word."

So, "Yes," Dallas said in response to my confession. "Being right is actually a very hard burden to be able to carry gracefully and humbly. That's why nobody likes to sit next to the kid in class who's right all the time. One of the hardest things in the world is to be right and not hurt other people with it."

Huh?

Over the years, that's the question I most frequently posed to Dallas. "Huh?" Sometimes we would speak together publicly, and my main job was to ask the same questions for others that I asked when it was just the two of us having a conversation.

"Hell is just the best God can do for some people."

Huh?

"I'm quite sure God will let everybody into heaven that can possibly stand it."

Huh?

"Your eternal destiny is not cosmic retirement; it is to be part of a tremendously creative project, under unimaginably splendid leadership, on an inconceivably vast scale, with ever-increasing cycles of fruitfulness and enjoyment—that is the prophetic vision which 'eye has not seen and ear has not heard.'"

Huh?

Sentences would come out of Dallas that simply couldn't come out of anyone else, and then he would leave them in your mind like little time-delay bombs for you to deal with when they go off.

I found myself moving from polite questions about church and ideas to the personal. That little house in Box Canyon began to change from a classroom into a confessional: Why is it so hard for me to love the actual people in my church? Why is it that I know I want to love my children, but I seem to be driven to be a success — especially in a vocation supposedly calling people to die to their need to be successful? Why do I get jealous of other pastors who are more successful than I am? Why am I never satisfied? Why do I feel a deep, secret loneliness? Why is it that I have a PhD in clinical psychology and a master of divinity and work as a pastor and yet I'm not sure who I am?

"The most important thing in your life," Dallas said, "is not what you do; it's who you become. That's what you will take into eternity. You are an unceasing spiritual being with an eternal destiny in God's great universe."

Huh?

"You are an unceasing spiritual being with an eternal destiny in God's great universe. That's the most important thing for you to know about you. You should write that down. You should repeat it regularly. Brother John, you think you have to be

> *The most important thing in your life is not what you do; it's who you become. That's what you will take into eternity.*
> **DALLAS WILLARD**

someplace else or accomplish something more to find peace. But it's right here. God has yet to bless anyone except where they actually are. Your soul is not just something that lives on after your body dies. It's the most important thing about you. It is your life."

Long pause.

When I thought about how my life was going, I always thought about my outer world. It is the world of reputation and appearance. It consists of how much I have and of what people think. It is visible and obvious. In my outer world, it is easy to keep score. I always thought that improving the circumstances of my outer world is what makes me feel happy inside.

But this was an invitation to another world — what Gordon MacDonald would call a "private world." It is unseen, unknown, hidden. It would garner no applause. It could be chaotic and dark and disordered, and no one might know. This house belonging to Dallas was where I would go to learn about this secret world.

It was a humble house, sweltering in the heat with an ancient air conditioner, piled high with books and papers and a few old pieces of furniture. The sign was invisible, and it would take years before I could read it: "Ye who enter here, enter upon holy ground." Wisdom, Knowledge, Faith, and Love had a home in Box Canyon after all.

Dallas once wrote about a tiny child who crept into his father's bedroom to sleep. In the dark, knowing his father was present was enough to take away his sense of aloneness. "Is your face turned toward me, Father?" he would ask. "Yes," his father replied. "My face is turned toward you." Only then could the child go to sleep.

Over the years I sought Dallas's wisdom to help me understand the human soul, and in this book I will share what I have learned. But I did not really just want to know about *any* soul. I wanted to know that *my* soul is not alone. I wanted to know that a face is turned toward it.

That's the journey we will take together.

PART 1

WHAT THE SOUL IS

CHAPTER 1

THE SOUL NOBODY KNOWS

One of the most important words in the Bible is *soul*. We throw that word around a lot, but if someone were to ask you to explain exactly what the word *soul* means, what would you say?

- *Why should I pay attention to my soul?*
- *Hasn't science disproven its existence?*
- *Isn't the soul the province of robe-wearing, herbal-tea drinkers?*
- *Isn't "soul-saving" old-fashioned language that ignores concerns for holistic justice?*
- *Won't it mean preoccupation with navel-gazing? Will I have to go to Big Sur or look some stranger in the eyes? Will I have to journal?*

Belief in the soul is ubiquitous: "Most people, at most times, in most places, at most ages, have believed that human beings have some kind of souls." We know it matters. We suspect it's important. But we're not sure what it means.

It's the word that won't go away, even though it is used less and less.

From birth to our final resting place ("May God rest his soul"), the soul is our earliest companion and our ultimate concern. The word is ethereal, mysterious, and deep. And a little spooky. ("All Souls' Day" comes two days after Halloween and has always sounded to me like disembodied spirits floating around at the Haunted Mansion in Disneyland.)

How many of our children learned this prayer? How many times have *you* recited it at bedtime?

> Now I lay me down to sleep,
> I pray the Lord my soul to keep.
> If I should die before I wake,
> I pray the Lord my soul to take.

Is it just me, or are those scary words to teach a seven-year-old to pray alone in the dark? I guess it's not just me: "That [prayer] so, so did not work for me...," wrote Anne Lamott. "Don't be taking my soul. You leave my soul right here, in my fifty-pound body."

What does it mean to ask God "my soul to keep"? If I expire before sunrise, and he takes my soul, what exactly is it that gets taken?

HOW MUCH DOES A SOUL WEIGH?

Jeffrey Boyd is a kind of Don Quixote of the soul. He is a Yale psychiatrist, an ordained minister, and coauthor of *Diagnostic and Statistical Manual of Mental Disorders*, a work in which you will search in vain for a single reference to "soul." It does include something called "depersonalization disorder," a feeling of estrangement from oneself. But Boyd also writes books and articles trying to reinject the word *soul* into our scientific vocabulary.

In one study of hundreds of church attenders, Boyd found that most people believe they know what *soul* means, but when asked to explain it, they can't do it. The soul turns out to be like Supreme Court Associate Justice Potter Stewart's description of obscenity: "It may be hard to define, but I know it when I see it." About half of church attenders adopt what Boyd calls the Looney Tunes Theory of the soul:

> If Daffy Duck were blown up with dynamite, then there would
> be a transparent image of Daffy Duck that would float up from
> the dead body. The translucent image would have wings and

carry a harp. From the air this apparition would speak down to Bugs Bunny, who set off the dynamite.

It sounds funny to talk about cartoons when it comes to the soul, but as Aristotle said, "The soul never thinks without a picture."

The soul can't be put under a microscope or studied by X-ray. About a hundred years ago a doctor measured the slight weight loss experienced by seven tuberculosis victims at the moment of death, which led him to claim that the soul weighs twenty-one grams. His idea years later created a title for a movie with Sean Penn and Naomi Watts, but it was never duplicated and was widely ridiculed in the medical community. Some are convinced that soul language needs to go.

A philosopher named Owen Flanagan says there is no place in science for the notion of a soul: "Desouling is the primary operation of the scientific image."

But Boyd argues that we see people who have a strength of soul that simply will not be degraded by the humiliation their body puts them through. He writes of a woman named Patricia who suffered from the effects of diabetes, a heart attack, and two strokes; she went blind, went into renal failure (which required dialysis), and had both her legs amputated—all while only in her thirties. She was placed in a nursing home, except for those several times a year when she had to be hospitalized, frequently going into a coma for one or two weeks during those stays.

Pat was part of a church in Washington, D.C., that wanted to create a homeless shelter. They could not find anyone with the leadership skills to pull it off, so she volunteered. In between dialysis and amputations and comas, she pulled together the team and got the zoning changes, architectural help, and fund-raising done. She then helped the team figure out the rules for the homeless people who used the shelter, and she recruited and trained the staff who ran it.

When Pat died after the shelter's first successful year in operation, homeless people stood next to U.S. Cabinet members such as Secretary of State James Baker at her funeral.

The soul knows a glory that the body cannot rob. In some ways, in some cases, the more the body revolts, the more the soul shines through. People may claim to believe that all you are is your body. But Pat said one time, "The only thing I can depend on with my body is that it will fail me. Somehow my body is mine, but it's not 'me.'"

Greatness of soul is available to people who do not have the luxury of being ecstatic about the condition and appearance of their bodies.

Greatness of soul is available to people who do not have the luxury of being ecstatic about the condition and appearance of their bodies.

THE HIGH AND THE LOW OF THE SOUL

We can't seem to talk about beauty or art without talking about the soul—particularly music. Aretha Franklin is the Queen of Soul. It is possible that if your soul isn't moved by Ray Charles, Otis Redding, Little Richard, Fats Domino, or James Brown, you may want to check to make sure you still have one. Kid Rock wrote "Rebel Soul." A sixteen-year-old, wanna-be pop singer named Jewel hitchhiked to Mexico and watched desperate people looking for help and wrote what would become her breakthrough song: "Who Will Save Your Soul?"

We need the word when we speak of not just the highest, but also the lowest parts of human existence. Over one hundred years ago, W.E.B. Du Bois called his book about the oppressed humanity of a race *The Souls of Black Folk*. No other word would do: *The Selves of Black Folk* does not carry the same dignity. "Soul food" would be the name given for Southern cooking that began with slaves who had to survive on whatever leftovers they were given. "Soul power" became the name for a sense of dignity and worth in a people who had been forced to live with neither. "Soul brother" reflects the bond that knits together those persecuted because of skin color.

Does soul require suffering to make itself known?

We speak of larger entities having soul. During every election, politicians and pundits warn us that the soul of America is at stake. ServiceMaster CEO William Pollard wrote a leadership book called *The Soul of the Firm*. (Can a cleaning company have a soul?) Shortstop and team captain Derek Jeter has been given the title "soul of the Yankees." Quarterback Tom Brady deemed receiver Wes Walker the "soul" of the New England Patriots. These may be metaphors, but they point to the notion of the soul as that which holds a larger entity together.

Why do the Chicago Cubs never get a soul?

SOUL FOR SALE

We speak of the soul as a source of strength, and yet we speak of it as fragile. Something about the soul always seems to be at risk. A soul is something that can be lost or sold. The selling of a soul has been made into countless operas, books, and country music lyrics, as well as a movie called *Bedazzled* and a musical called *Damn Yankees*. Jonathon Moulton, a New Hampshire brigadier general in the 1700s, sold his soul to the Devil (according to legend) to have his boots filled with gold coins monthly when he hung them by the fireplace. In the television series *The Simpsons*, Homer sells his soul for a donut and then impulsively eats all but one bite, which he puts in the refrigerator with the instructions: "Soul Donut. Do Not Eat."

Periodically somebody tries to sell their soul on eBay. Most recently a woman named Lori N. offered hers for $2,000 after a car accident left her strapped for cash. No takers, though. It turns out eBay has a "no soul-selling" policy that allows them to stay neutral on the existence of souls: If souls don't exist, they don't allow the selling of nonexistent items; if souls do exist, they don't allow people to sell themselves off one part at a time. The real problem, they say, is that if you sell something on eBay, you have to be in position to deliver what you sell. If you could buy a soul through anybody, it would probably be Ikea — Swedes will sell pretty much anything—but then you would have to take it home and assemble it yourself from instructions that make no sense at all.

Souls keep popping up in our most loved stories. Harry Potter is a teenage wizard with a chosen destiny to overthrow the evil dark wizard, Voldemort, who murdered his parents. Harry discovers deep connections of the soul with the Dark Lord. The greatest sin, murder, is discovered to tear the soul asunder, damage that can only be healed by honest remorse. The Dementor's kiss is a fate worse than death—to have one's soul removed by a soulless creature. To live without a soul is worse than not living. "Have you no soul?" is really another way of saying, "Is it possible that your mind with its values and conscience are not even troubled by what your will has chosen and your body carried out?"

Does a fetus have a soul? A whole debate about abortion rages around this. Does life happen at conception? Is that when a being becomes human? Plato believed souls were reincarnated based on how elevated they were last time around: wise souls come back as seekers of beauty or kings or athletic trainers, whereas cowards come back as women and boozers may come back as donkeys. Augustine said that maybe souls preexist somewhere and then slip into bodies on their own, like people picking out a good car.

We are not sure what the soul is, but the word sells. Advertisers speak of cars being soulful; Kia actually manufactures a car called the Kia Soul. Is it for people who want to go beyond transportation to transmigration? You can also find the Soul Diva (for the "style conscious woman who regards her car as important as her entire outfit"); the Soul Burner (the "bad boy" of the Soul concept); and the Soul Searcher (for the driver focused on "achieving personal inner peace and creating a calm cocoon for occupants").

Maybe that's my problem: when I was growing up, we had a Rambler.

The word *soul* won't go away, because it speaks somehow of eternity:

> Now there are some things we all know, but we don't take'em
> out and look at'm very often. We all know that *something* is

eternal. And it ain't houses and it ain't names and it ain't earth, and it ain't even the stars.... everybody knows in their bones that *something* is eternal, and that something has to do with human beings. All the greatest people ever lived have been telling us that for five thousand years and yet you'd be surprised how people are always losing hold of it.

A movie called *The Sixth Sense* starring Bruce Willis tells of a little boy cursed with the gift of seeing dead people. A huge twist comes at the end of the movie; I don't want to spoil it for you, but Bruce Willis, much to his surprise, turns out to be one of the dead people. A kind of mirror image to the story—and maybe the eeriest of all psychological diagnoses—is a condition known as "Cotard's syndrome."

Named for the French neurologist who described it in the 1880s, Cotard's syndrome ranges from claims that central organs are missing to the belief that one is already dead. It's sometimes called Walking Corpse Syndrome. Jules Cotard described a woman he called Mademoiselle X, who claimed that God did not exist and that her soul did not exist and that she was nothing more than a decomposing body. Eventually she died of starvation—which must have come as a great shock to her. In one condition, a soul is dead but thinks it's alive; in the other, the soul is alive but believes it's dead.

> In one condition, a soul is dead but thinks it's alive; in the other, the soul is alive but believes it's dead.

Are souls reserved for humans? If a computer were able to think—could it have a soul? Stanford professor Clifford Nass wrote the book *The Man Who Lied to His Laptop*. He has found that human beings treat computers the same way we treat people—we are flattered by their praise; we want to please them; we will even lie to them to avoid hurting their feelings. Could a computer be able to love a family, or enjoy a sunset, or grow in humility? What about souls and technology? Aristotle said that a friend is one soul in two bodies. Would the same thing be true of somebody if you cloned them?

A WINDOW TO YOUR SOUL

We speak of the eyes being the window to the soul. Scientists say the eyes can reveal our inner thoughts. For instance, when people are doing hard mental work, their pupils dilate. Daniel Kahneman wrote about researchers monitoring the eyes of subjects trying to solve difficult math problems. They would sometimes surprise subjects by asking them, "Why did you give up just now?"

"How did you know?" the unsuspecting students would ask.

"We have a window to your soul."

Psychologist Edmund Hess writes how pupils widen when people look at beautiful nature pictures. When I was in grad school, I saw two famous pictures of a lovely woman — identical, except that in one of them, her pupils are dilated, and that picture is always judged much more attractive. Belladonna, an herb-based drug that expands the pupils, is actually sold as a cosmetic. Professional poker players sometimes wear sunglasses simply to keep their pupils from giving their excitement away.

U.S. President George W. Bush said that when he looked into Russian President Vladimir Putin's eyes, he was able to get a sense of his soul. Senator John McCain later said that when he looked into Putin's eyes, he saw three letters: "A K and a G and a B" (a reference to the former Soviet security agency).

My first date with the woman who would become my wife did not begin well. She actually fell asleep. But it was the last ten minutes that turned things around, when we talked to each other, and (she told me later) I made great eye contact. She told me she thought that was sexy. Can a soul be sexy?

We can't talk about our work without talking about our souls, although they often seem at odds. A "soulful work" movement suggests that while cubicles and monitors make us more efficient, our souls lose something when disconnected from the rhythms of working outdoors, of making things with our own hands. And the Internet is full of lists of the ten or twenty most soul-crushing jobs in the world, such as "Jobs that make you feel like a caged ADHD

Chihuahua on Red Bull." Maybe there should be a Take Your Soul to Work Day.

When we talk of love, we speak of soul. No one searches for the love of their life on a site called BodyMate.com. In his dialogue *The Symposium*, Plato has Aristophanes present the story of soul mates. Aristophanes states that humans originally had four arms, four legs, and a single head made of two faces, but Zeus feared their power and split them all in half, condemning them to spend their lives searching for the other half to complete them. In the film *Jerry Maguire*, Tom Cruise's character expresses the idea unforgettably to Renée Zellweger: "You complete me." Can one person really complete another? Do we all have one and only one soul mate out there in the world someplace?

Churches are supposed to know about souls. We often sing a song that originated as a psalm: "Bless the Lord, O My Soul." How can your soul bless, or make happy, the Lord? Sometimes we speak of souls as if they are spiritual scalps: certain people who are highly regarded as "soul-winners" or who are especially adept at going after "lost souls." We get teary-eyed at the evangelist who desires to win "just one more soul for Jesus." Old-time evangelist Billy Sunday used to calculate how much money it cost him to save a soul: in Boston in 1911 it was $450. Churches did the job more economically: Congregationalists came in at $70 per soul, Baptists at $70, and Methodists at a staggeringly low $3.12 — which was cheap even by the 1911 standards!

The universal distress signal, SOS, is said to stand for "Save Our Souls." What does it mean for a soul to be saved?

"I don't deserve a soul, yet I still have one," writes Douglas Coupland. "I know because it hurts."

Remember that woman named Pat whose body betrayed a glorious soul? What Jeffrey Boyd did not write in that particular account is that Pat was his wife. Watching her body crumble, he watched something deeper than a body shine. He wrote in another place, "If a child is born with such withered legs that there will never be a possibility of walking or crawling, [is] the child's soul

*If a child is born
with such withered
legs that there
will never be a
possibility of walking
or crawling, [is] the
child's soul limited by
these architectural
disasters of the spine,
pelvis and femurs?*
JEFFREY BOYD

limited by these architectural disasters of the spine, pelvis and femurs? I had a son born with precisely these deformities. His name was Justin. That son also died."

We search for the soul because we're curious. But not just that. The search for the soul always begins with our great hurt.

If I should die before I wake, I pray the Lord my soul to take . . .

What is the soul?

CHAPTER 2

WHAT IS
THE SOUL?

I went to pick up Dallas Willard on a typical Chicago day in February when the roads were covered with salt trying to melt the ice, but the snow was coming down so fast you could hardly see the car in front of you. I was driving my ancient Toyota Corolla, in which the alignment was so out of whack that when I went over forty miles per hour, the car shook as if it had palsy and pulled to the left. Because of an earlier accident, the seat belt on the passenger side had to be threaded through the armrest to hold the door closed.

"Sorry about the car," I offered, though I thought Dallas wouldn't even notice. He was a little grayer since I had last seen him. I had moved from California to Chicago two years earlier, but he had agreed to talk with me monthly by phone. Eventually he came to Chicago to speak at our church.

We chatted while we drove — very slowly — to lunch. Every once in a while Dallas would absentmindedly start singing a hymn, such as "Rock of Ages" or "Leaning on the Everlasting Arms," and I would join in. He used to lead music as well as preach at the little Baptist churches he served in the hills of Missouri.

We pulled into a Chili's and sat down at a table. Having not been with him in a while, I was reminded again of how at ease he was with himself. He was the same person, whether he was talking to an assistant janitor or a famous leader. When Dallas finished speaking at a conference, people would line up to talk with him, and he always obliged them. It's not just that he didn't hurry through those conversations; he genuinely didn't seem to want to hurry. The clear impression I got was not that Dallas was working hard to be patient. It was as though impatience and worry were simply not in his body. He had an inner life that seemed at peace with the life everyone else sees.

I wanted to know that kind of inner life.

THIS TINY, FRAGILE, VULNERABLE, PRECIOUS THING ABOUT YOU

We each have an outer life and an inner one. My outer self is the public, visible me. My accomplishments, my work, and my reputation lie there. My outer world had changed a great deal since I had last seen Dallas. I was working at a church that—in the little world of my profession—was large and visible. There were more people on staff at this church than there were attendees at the church where I had last worked. Suddenly people sought out my opinion more and assumed I was smarter than I was and invited me to speak at their events. My outer world was now larger and busier and more complex than it had ever been.

But my inner world had not grown at all. My inner life is where my secret thoughts and hopes and wishes live. Because my inner life is invisible, it is easy to neglect. No one has direct access to it, so it wins no applause. Abraham Lincoln was a brilliant lawyer, but notoriously disorganized; he used to have a bulging folder labeled, "If you can't find it anywhere else, look here." My private self can begin to look as chaotic and untended as the inside of Lincoln's folder.

I thought that such a large change in my outer world would bring a quick upgrade to my inner one—more fulfillment, more gratification. Instead, the very busy-ness and complexity of it was almost like a private blizzard that made it hard to navigate my internal world clearly.

What drew me to Dallas was the sense that here was someone who had mastered the inner life—or had at least gone much farther down that road than most. There was leisure of spirit to him. It sounds strange to say, but he had an overwhelmingly calm face.

I asked him, "Why am I not happier, now that I'm getting to do what is in many ways a dream job?" I asked him, "How can I have a private self that is flourishing no matter what my public self is doing?"

For that, Dallas said, we would have to talk about the care of the soul. I was afraid that topic might come up.

"I work at a church where my job involves saving souls," I began. "But if someone asked me, I'd have a hard time saying exactly what a soul is. Is *soul* just a word religious people throw around?"

I wasn't prepared for his answer.

"Brother John, why is there such value and mystery to your existence? The really deep reason is because of this tiny, fragile, vulnerable, precious thing about you called your *soul*. You are not just a self; you are a soul. 'The LORD God formed man of the dust of

> *You're a soul made by God, made for God, and made to need God, which means you were not made to be self-sufficient.*
> **DALLAS WILLARD**

the ground, and breathed into his nostrils the breath of life; and man became a living soul.' You're a soul made by God, made for God, and made to need God, which means you were not made to be self-sufficient."

In one of his books, Dallas has further explained,

What is running your life at any given moment is your soul. Not external circumstances, not your thoughts, not your intentions, not even your feelings, but your soul. The soul is that aspect of your whole being that correlates, integrates, and enlivens everything going on in the various dimensions of the self. The soul is the life center of human beings.

THE LIFE CENTER OF HUMAN BEINGS

I thought I knew what Dallas meant. Sometimes I will watch the sun set at the beach while I smell the saltwater and listen to the crashing surf; or I will be standing on a ledge along the Big Sur overlooking a mountain range and feel this enormous combination of joy and awe. There is a depth to those moments that goes beyond a body. Your soul connects your thoughts and your sensations and your gratitude and your will and sends a message to your entire being. You can send that message to other persons; you can send it to God. You can say "Wow!" to the universe. That is the soul at work.

"Anytime you want to care for something, you have to understand it, whether it's a beagle or a BMW," Dallas continued. "Take that high-performance automobile you were driving. [Oops! He had noticed after all.] If a car is tuned and fueled and oiled and aligned, it is capable of amazing things — even *your* car," he said, smiling. "If you do not understand its parts and how they work — well, we see the result."

Dallas went on to make the obvious connection. He said it is terribly important to understand the "parts" of the inner life. Each one must be healthy and working as God intended it to work. If your soul is healthy, no external circumstance can destroy your life. If your soul is unhealthy, no external circumstance can redeem your life.

But what exactly *is* the soul?

Dallas took a napkin and drew the first of a series of concentric circles. The innermost circle, according to Dallas, is the human will — your capacity to choose. You can say, "Yes," and you can say, "No." The will is what makes you a person and not a thing. It's what the Bible is talking about when it says God made people to "exercise dominion." The will is something we treasure greatly in ourselves and others.

But if the will is so central, why isn't spiritual life a lot easier? Why can't I simply tell people to use their will to do what God says or to feel God's presence?

"The will is very central, but it's also incredibly limited," Dallas explained. "Do you ever find yourself doing something that goes against your better judgment or values?"

"Hardly ever," I said as I finished my second piece of molten hot fudge cake and ice cream.

"The will is very good at making simple and large commitments like getting married, or deciding to move someplace," Dallas explained. "But it is very bad at trying to override habits and patterns and attitudes that are deeply rooted in us. If you try to improve your soul by willpower, you will exhaust yourself and everyone around you."

Why is that? Dallas drew a second circle around the first to illustrate.

"The next part of the person is the mind. In the ancient world, the mind referred to both a person's thoughts and their feelings. By thoughts I mean all the ways a person is conscious of things."

That made a lot of sense to me. Thoughts and feelings are flowing through us all the time, mostly flowing in habitual patterns that willpower alone cannot sustainably redirect. When I think thoughts that are false or unworthy, when I entertain desires that are in opposition to what God wants for my life, I damage my soul. The apostle Paul says, "The mind of sinful man is death, but the mind controlled by the Spirit is life and peace."

The mind craves to be at peace.

Dallas drew another circle that he said represents our bodies. "The body is our little kingdom. That's the one place in all the universe where our tiny wills have a chance to be in charge. Imagine for a moment you had a will and a mind but no body."

Huh?

"Our bodies are like our little 'power packs.' We couldn't be us without them. They are filled with all kinds of appetites and all kinds of habits. In a way, we 'outsource' behaviors from tying our shoelaces, to driving a car, to our bodies, so that our wills and our minds don't have to worry about them. Our bodies are amazing. But they are not the whole story. I am not just the stuff my body is made of."

He drew another circle, and this one, he said, represents the soul.

Soul

Body

Mind

Will

THE OPERATING SYSTEM OF YOUR LIFE

"The soul is the capacity to integrate all the parts into a single, whole life. It is something like a program that runs a computer; you don't usually notice it unless it messes up."

> The soul is the capacity to integrate all the parts into a single, whole life.
> **DALLAS WILLARD**

According to Dallas, the soul seeks harmony, connection, and integration. That is why *integrity* is such a deep soul-word. The human soul seeks to integrate our will and our mind and our body into an integral person. Beyond that, the soul seeks to connect us with other people, with creation, and with God himself—who made us to be rooted in him the way a tree is rooted by a life-giving stream.

Dallas helped me understand what I have wondered over the

years about the soul. It is the deepest part of you, and it is the whole person. This is so true that the word *soul*, in both the Old and New Testaments and elsewhere in the ancient world, is often simply a synonym for the person. Even in our day it is interesting how our language reflects this. Questions on airplane or ship records sometimes ask, "How many souls on board?" Most people have no idea where this comes from, but it traces its origins to the ancient world. For example, in Acts 27:37, Luke reports on a shipwreck involving the apostle Paul: "And we were all in the ship two hundred threescore and sixteen [276] souls."

Your soul is what integrates your will (your intentions), your mind (your thoughts and feelings, your values and conscience), and your body (your face, body language, and actions) into a single life. A soul is healthy—well-ordered—when there is harmony between these three entities and God's intent for all creation. When you are connected with God and other people in life, you have a healthy soul.

UNHEALTHY SOULS

Therefore, according to Dallas, an unhealthy soul is one that experiences *dis-integration*, and sin always causes the disintegration of the soul. As Leonard Cohen put it, "The blizzard of the world has crossed the threshold, and it has overturned the order of the soul." A few years ago I was asked to speak at the church of a pastor in the Deep South whose success had made him famous. Pictures of him with famous people and framed covers of his best-selling books lined his office walls. But now he was beyond the age when most people retire, his church was shrinking, his influence was waning, and he was miserable.

When I met this pastor, he began to tell me how wrong his critics were, even though I hardly knew him or his critics. He chastised his people for not bringing enough visitors to fill the empty seats. "I'm tired of looking at empty seats," he said, as if the goal of church is empty-seat avoidance. He had climbed to remarkable heights in church ministry, but his mind was preoccupied by bitter thoughts. His face attempted smiles that were disconnected from his feelings, and his will strained to maintain a façade that had been hollowed out long ago.

His soul was *dis*-integrating.

I thought of another man, a businessman who devoted his life to making money. His children always knew that they had less priority than his job. He never said so, of course, but our deepest devotions simply leak out of our bodies by how we spend our time and what makes us smile and what claims our energy. The man built a corporate empire, but his employees all felt used.

He and his wife bought a magnificent home overlooking the ocean in Southern California. He had a stroke, yet no one came to visit him. He sits in a wheelchair now, breathing from an oxygen tank, alone in a mansion cage.

He still obsesses over what he owns and remains incapable of gratitude or generosity.

This is the ruined soul.

When I think of that pastor and this businessman, I recall Jesus' memorable words about the soul: "What does it profit a man to gain the whole world and forfeit his soul?" I have always thought this verse meant that in the long run it won't do you any good to acquire a lot of money and have a lot of sex and other sensual pleasures if you end up going to hell.

When I mentioned that to Dallas, he gently corrected me: "That is *not* what Jesus is saying. Jesus is not talking here about people going to hell."

He explained that Jesus is talking about a diagnosis, not a destination. If we think of hell as a torture chamber and heaven as a pleasure factory, we will never understand Jesus' point. For the ruined soul—that is, where the will and the mind and the body are disintegrated, disconnected from God, and living at odds with the way God made life in the universe to run—acquiring the whole world could not even produce satisfaction, let alone meaning and goodness.

To lose my soul means I no longer have a healthy center that organizes and guides my life. I am a car without a steering wheel.

It doesn't matter how fast I can go, because I am a crash waiting to happen.

Farmers in the Midwest used to run a rope from their house to the barn at the first sight of a blizzard. They knew stories of people who had died in their own yards during a whiteout because they couldn't find their way home. Parker Palmer writes that the "blizzard of the world" is the fear and frenzy and deceit and indifference to the suffering of others that separates us from our own souls and our moral bearings. What we need, he said, is a rope from the back door to the barn so we can find our way home again. "When we catch sight of the soul, we can survive the blizzard without losing our hope or our way."

You don't have to believe the Bible to believe this. Just look around you.

A mom struggles to create the perfect home. Her husband does not help much. She doesn't tell him how much she resents it, mostly because she's always been afraid of conflict. She is angry at her children for not being perfect, for not being on track to get into the right school, for not making her look good as a mom. She is angry at her body for aging; feeling attractive has been the one unforced sense of worth in her life, and it is ebbing away. She withdraws. She drinks a little too much. She gossips with her friends about her other friends. She finds ways to fill time.

She thinks that her problem is her husband, or her kids, or her age, but it's not. It is her soul.

I don't mean to be unkind. Only God knows, with any given individual, what battles they may have fought with addiction or biology or abuse or simply temptations that I have never known. The point is that what Jesus said is true: gaining the outside world doesn't help you if your inside world collapses. Look at me. Look at you.

We live on the planet of lost souls. That is the human problem. It is not some superficial thing that only relates to getting the right afterlife if you affirm the right doctrines. It has to do with the depth of the human condition, which Jesus identified as nobody else ever has.

THE NEGLECTED SOUL DOESN'T GO AWAY; IT GOES AWRY

Our world has replaced the word *soul* with the word *self*, and they are not the same thing. The more we focus on our selves, the more we neglect our souls.

The word *psychologist* comes from the Greek word *psyche*, which actually means "soul." That ought to be what psychology is about, apart from what anyone thinks about religion. Sigmund Freud wrote that "Treatment of the psyche means . . . treatment of the soul. One could also understand it to mean treatment of sickness when it occurs in the life of the soul."

But psychology has focused on the self, and self carries a totally different connotation than soul. To focus on my soul means to look at my life under the care and connection of God. To focus on myself apart from God means losing awareness of what matters most.

The *Journal of the American Medical Association* cited a study that indicates that in the twentieth century, people who lived in each generation were three times more likely to experience depression than folks in the generation before them. Despite the rise of the mental health profession, people are becoming increasingly vulnerable to depression. Why? Martin Seligman, a brilliant psychologist with no religious ax to grind, has a theory that it's because we have replaced church, faith, and community with a tiny little unit that cannot bear the weight of meaning. That's the self. We're all about the self. We revolve our lives around ourselves.

Ironically, the more obsessed we are with our selves, the more we neglect our souls.

All of our language reflects this. If you're empty, you need to fulfill *yourself*. If you're stressed, learn how to take care of *yourself*. If you're on a job interview, you have to believe in *yourself*. If you're at the tattoo parlor, you must learn to express *yourself*. If someone dares to criticize you, you have to love *yourself*. If you're not getting your own way, you have to stand up for *yourself*. What should you do on a date? You ought to be *yourself*.

What if your *self* is a train wreck? What do you do then?

Self is a stand-alone, do-it-yourself unit, while the *soul* reminds us we were not made for ourselves. The soul always exists before God. So soul is needed for deep art, poetry, and music. Former opera singer Scott Flaherty said it best: "I mean, when you sing you're giving voice to your soul." Imagine singing, "Then sings my *self*, my Savior God to thee," or "Jesus, lover of my *self*." Innately we know that the self is not the soul, even as we do everything we can to preserve it.

ATTENDING TO THE SOUL

Every now and then I try to get away to the ocean and spend most of a day alone. It's a strange thing I don't fully understand. I have a lot of people in my life who love me and will tell me so, but when I am alone for an extended period of time, all the obligations and expectations and need to perform kind of melt from my mind. I am reminded when I'm alone that God loves me — that there is something about life that is infinitely deeper than all the expectations and roles and performance stuff of my outer life. It changes my body. I can feel it. My soul feels its worth.

You are only able to live in a way that really helps and loves others when your soul feels its worth. Yet we often pay far more attention to our work or our bodies or our finances than to our souls. But the soul is what we will take into eternity.

> *You are only able to live in a way that really helps and loves others when your soul feels its worth.*

Attending to the soul doesn't mean we neglect those practical things like career or health. The soul lies at the center of them all. It means I don't simply ask, "How can I be more successful in my work?" or "How can I acquire more money?" Instead, I learn to understand how my involvement in each area of life is marking my soul.

In fact, your soul can be all right when everything in your world is all wrong. Consider these marvelous words from Peter to a little flock: "Though you have not seen him [Jesus], you love him; and even though you do not see him now, you believe in him and are filled with an inexpressible and glorious joy, for you are receiving the end result of your faith, the salvation of your souls."

The salvation of your soul is not just about where you go when you die. The word *salvation* means healing or deliverance at the deepest level of who we are in the care of God through the presence of Jesus. Sooner or later, your world will fall apart. What will matter then is the soul you have constructed.

Horatio Spafford invested most of what he had in real estate. He lived in Chicago and lost everything in the Great Chicago Fire of 1871. It destroyed his home. They had no insurance. He lost most of his money. In 1873 he put his wife and their four daughters (their son having died of scarlet fever in 1870) on a ship heading to England as he stayed behind to restimulate his business. A few days after the ship departed, he received a telegram from his wife: "Saved alone. What shall I do?" There had been a shipwreck. All four of their daughters perished. Horatio quickly boarded another ship to England, and as it passed over the very same place in the ocean where his daughters had drowned, he wrote these words to as song:

> When peace, like a river, attendeth my way,
> When sorrows like sea billows roll;
> Whatever my lot, Thou hast taught me to say,
> It is well, it is well with my soul.

When Dallas and I left Chili's, it had stopped snowing. On our way home, I sang that song with Dallas. Many years later, on another voyage, in his home in Box Canyon, we would sing it again.

So what makes it well with my soul?

CHAPTER 3

A SOUL-CHALLENGED WORLD

I am interviewing Dallas at an event called Catalyst West. The church world has its own subculture of events and rhythms and networks. If you are a young leader in that world, you know of a conference called Catalyst, a gathering begun several years ago in Atlanta that exploded so in popularity that a West Coast version was needed a few years later.

This one is taking place in Irvine, California. Thousands of young pastors and wanna-be pastors and musicians and artists are in a room with fog machines and lighting artistry and sound systems that make it kind of a twenty-first-century, evangelical, indoors Woodstock. I feel like I am the oldest person in the room, culturally if not chronologically (Dallas being twenty years older than I). Dallas wears a jacket and tie. It is for him — the boy who could not afford socks in college — a gesture of respect for his audience. No one else in the room wears a tie. No one else in the room owns a tie. No one else in the room would know how to tie a tie.

On the stage I ask Dallas questions about ministry. His response: "What matters is not the accomplishments you achieve; what matters is the person you become."

Huh?

He speaks of eternity, and how the soul is formed, and how temptation works, and why sin is so destructive. He speaks of the slow, unglamorous building of character. I worry about how this is going. Other speakers at this event speak with great passion, while Dallas speaks in the cultivated monotone of an academic. Other speakers tell dramatic stories of radical devotion and hellish suffering, but Dallas tells no stories at all.

When he is done, the whole crowd of twenty-something, tattooed clergy dudes leap to their feet. Dallas is presented with a kind of Lifetime Achievement Award. They cheer as if he's Jack Nicholson at the Oscars. I am at a loss to account for this response. And then it occurs to me:

The soul searches for a father.

SOUL-DAMAGED LIVING IN A SOUL-CHALLENGED WORLD

Consider these vignettes from people trying to survive:

Success Man. When I was young, I had finished college and started life. I was married; I had children. I got a job as a financial analyst for an investment firm in Manhattan. I monitored the world. Currencies were my specialty: I would place bets on when the yen was going up and when the euro was going down. I had monitors that kept me in touch with every time zone every hour of the day. My cell was on vibrate twenty-four hours a day, because a window can open and close at any time.

My boss was a remarkable man—one of the inventors of the hedge fund, which can enable investors to make money on anything whether the price goes up or down. Everybody who worked in the firm was twenty years younger than he was. We would sometimes sleep on cots in our offices to be able to pull the trigger on deals in a heartbeat. I got more money for Christmas bonuses than my dad ever dreamed of making in a lifetime.

My family lived in an apartment not far from Central Park. The kids went to a private school we could barely afford. We bought a place in the suburbs that we could escape to on weekends. I would wake up at 5:00 a.m. and start a coffee IV and live on adrenaline all day. My wife did most of the day-to-day stuff with the kids; we had a kind of Inside/Outside arrangement where I was Mr. Outside. I had only one secret.

I heard voices. One voice actually. It came at random. I could never make out what it was saying. Whenever it spoke, something else was going on, or someone else was making noise, or I was on my way somewhere.

It bothered me, but I could not figure it out. When I would be still to try to catch it, I heard nothing. It was like footsteps behind a character in a movie; as soon as the character stops to see if they really are footsteps, the footsteps stop too.

One day, when I got home from work, I heard it clearly.

I am your soul. And I am dying.

I did not hear it again for many years.

Not-So-Successful Woman. I am in a seventh-grade algebra class, sitting next to a boy who is smarter than me. During a test, I sneak a look at his paper. Not enough to get caught — once or twice, enough to help me move up to an A-minus. I don't really think about whether or not I deserve this grade, or if what I am doing is fair to other students. I know that if I get a good grade, I will be happy and my parents will be proud. I dimly tell myself that because I really did study, and because most of the questions I answer myself, it's not really cheating. I have done this before. Outside of the risk of getting caught, it doesn't really bother me.

I am playing in the finals of a tennis tournament. I come to the net, and my opponent hits a lob over my head. I call it out, though it was not. There is an umpire at the net who doesn't initiate calls, but is available to arbitrate. My opponent trusts me; she doesn't question my call. The umpire, whom I know, looks at me after the point. Does he know? I feel queasy. Is it because I cheated, or because I think he knows? How much better would I feel if I had simply cheated and no one had noticed? How much worse would I feel if everyone knew — not just that the call was wrong, but that I had done it deliberately?

My mother and my father achieved so much that I could never

compete. I was never the pretty one, or the smart one, or the talented one; I just filled out the family roster. Now I am married, but my marriage brings me little pleasure. My husband is as committed to his career as he is passive at home. I want to scream at him sometimes because anything would be better than his shallowness and silence. I tried teaching, but don't do it well. I have tried writing, but every rejection from every publisher is so painful that I can't bring myself to risk it again.

I work at a job I do not like that does not challenge me, and I feel buried. My two daughters struggle with not being liked by boys and not having the right appearance. When I see other parents at school or at church with children who look successful and happy, for whom life and school and athletics come easily, I find myself feeling furious with them and with God and myself. I am not an alcoholic, but I look forward to three glasses of wine at night so I can finally feel relief from this knot in my gut. I do not expect that my life will ever be any different.

Famous Man. One of the most successful television shows of all-time recorded its final episode. Its star, Ray Romano, had ridden its popularity from struggling stand-up comedy to fabulous wealth and staggering fame. He lived in his parents' basement until he was twenty-nine years old; by the end of his sitcom's run he had become the highest paid actor per episode in television history. After filming the last show, he stood before the studio audience and reviewed how his life had changed and who he had become. When he had moved to New York nine years earlier, he said, his big brother Richard had tucked a note into his luggage. Ray read it, in tears, to the audience: "What does it profit a man if he gains the whole world and loses his soul?"

Preacher Man. I begin a new job at a church. Another man on staff is a year younger, a musician who works in the worship area. He is a rock star. When he's on the platform, the house goes crazy. When he leads a worship concert, the place is packed. When he finishes, people are on their feet applauding and stomping; they won't let him stop. It's all anyone can talk about. I am consumed with the realization that I wish it were me they were clapping for. I realize I'm working at a church. I'm aware of how ludicrous it is that my job is to teach people to follow somebody who said, "Die to yourself and follow me," yet I'm jealous of someone because he's better at calling people to die to themselves than I am. But those thoughts are still present, and I can't wish them away. If I can shine brightly when I get my chance, I will feel better.

I tell an acquaintance a story about a third person we both know that will put that person in a bad light. I get a twinge of pleasure out of this. I don't know why.

I count up how many dollars I have accumulated for something I want to buy. I don't count up how many dollars I have accumulated to be able to give to people who are dying of hunger. I rarely think or feel guilty about this.

I come home from a party. When we pull into the driveway, my wife puts her hand on my arm and says gently, "I noticed when we were with other people today, you didn't look them in the eye very much. People love it when you look at them; it's what made me begin to love you in the first place. I think you should work at it."

My first thought is: who died and made *you* body language queen? I am Swedish, my people are Swedish—we never look anyone in the eyes. Not even the eye doctor.

I withdraw from her. I lean more toward my side of the car. I get quiet, polite, distant. You learn, when you are married, how to send signals that will register deep in the soul yet are subtle enough to offer plausible deniability.

Then I think of how I told God I would like to be in training to love people better. I think of how I want to be remembered when I reach the end of my life. I would like to have looked deeply into many eyes; to connect deeply with many souls; to have people know that I noticed them and cared about them and actually loved them.

Something in my heart turns and melts a little. And I say to my wife, "Thank you for telling me that. Thank you for having the

The most important thing about you is not the things that you achieve; it is the person that you become.
DALLAS WILLARD

courage to love me that much." And somewhere in the universe something heals — and that something is a tiny little tear in my soul.

These are the cries of the soul, including my own. All of them — and a million others — are real and are what matter deeply about us.

"The most important thing about you," Dallas would often say, "is not the things that you achieve; it is the person that you become."

A PARABLE OF THE SOUL

Our problem is that this world does not teach us to pay attention to what matters. We circulate résumés that chronicle what we have accomplished, not who we have become. The advertisements we watch, the conversations we hold, the criteria by which we are judged, and the entertainment we consume all inflame our desire to change our situation, while God waits to redeem our souls.

How does the world we live in keep us from attending to our souls?

Jesus told a story about this. It's of such importance that this story is the first of his recorded in the gospel of Mark and the one parable he fully interpreted to his disciples.

It's a story about seeds, a sower, and some soil. In a story like this one, it helps to notice what are the constants and what are the variables in order to understand Jesus' point.

The seed is a constant. This is not a good story about good seeds and bad seeds. The seed will take root given half a chance. The seed is a little picture of God's desire and action to redeem souls.

The sower is a constant. This isn't a story about good sowers and bad sowers. The first thing we notice about him is how generous he is with the seed. He scatters it everywhere.

It is the soil that gets interesting. The soil is the variable. And for "soil," we might replace it with the word *soul*. The closed soul is death. The receptive soul is life.

The Hardened Soul. Some seeds fall on the path, Jesus said. In the Middle East, conditions are already dry. The path is the place where farmers walk, where sheep make their way to water and grass. The path is hard and dry, and the seeds don't have a chance.

Souls get that way.

Often these seeds are people who have been hurt or disappointed. They form a protective shell. They become cynical or bitter or suspicious. Often in the Scriptures these are brothers. Cain may have been the first hardened soul; his brother Abel had a sacrifice accepted by God, but his was not. Jacob is hardened against Esau. David is estranged from his brothers, and the same thing happens among his sons. Joseph's brothers hardened against him because they saw that their father loved him and not them — they hated him. When he told them about his dreams, they hated him all the more. Their minds were filled with anger, their feelings were envious, their wills became hostile, and their hands betrayed him. Then they lied to their father; they rationalized their actions. Their hardened souls were lost.

The world diverts my soul-attention when it encourages me to think of myself more as a victim than as a human. I am so wrapped up in the hurt I have received that I do not notice the hurt I inflict.

I have a friend who has not spoken to her sister for fifteen years. They had a falling-out over their parents' will, over a tiny amount of money. There are only two churches in town, so one of them had to become Episcopalian. They pray every week, "And forgive us our debts as we forgive our debtors" (even though the Episcopalian had to switch "debts" to "transgressions"). But in a world where victimhood has become status, souls go unexamined for hardness.

Sometimes the smallest acts of sacrifice or self-denial can break up hard soil. A friend of mine sent me a few sentences from an article she saw online on "How to Stay Christian in College":

> ... make small sacrifices. Make a vow to wake up and go to breakfast every morning, even if your first class isn't until eleven a.m. Choose a plain cheese pizza rather than pepperoni.

You'll be surprised how these tiny sacrifices work an interior magic, shifting your focus ever so slightly away from yourself. Once you're a little bit to the side, God can come to the center.

Underneath the hardness is often fear. The fear of being rejected. The fear of looking foolish. The fear of being hurt. The fear of broken pride. But souls can be saved when the soil gets soft.

It takes a little, just a tiny little bit of softness in the soil to give the seed a chance. The seed is strong—stronger than you can imagine. One tiny seed can break up a sidewalk if it can find a little room to breathe.

The hardened soul is more vulnerable to being saved than it knows.

The Shallow Soul. Some of the seed fell on rocky soil. The idea here is not that there was a bunch of rocks, but that there was only a thin layer of topsoil with solid rock underneath. The seed had life until the sun came out. But the life withers quickly, Jesus said, because the soil is too shallow for roots.

The world conspires against our souls, keeping our lives superficial.

"Superficiality," said Richard Foster, "is the curse of our age." The desperate need of the soul is not for intelligence, nor talent, nor yet excitement; just depth. This is the cry of one of the great soul songs of the Psalms: "As the deer pants for streams of water, so my soul pants for you.... Why, my soul, are you downcast?... Deep calls to deep in the roar of your waterfalls."

Superficiality is the curse of our age.
RICHARD FOSTER

The soul is the deepest part of you. It is so deep that there are parts to my soul I cannot seem to understand or control. This is why writers in the ancient world, not just in the Bible, would often address the soul in the third person, in a way they would never do with the will or the mind or the body. There is a depth to your soul that is beyond words.

Nancy and I got married in California. Nancy was a California girl, but I wanted to bring joy to her soul, so for a surprise, I took her to Wisconsin for our honeymoon. It did *not* bring joy to her soul, so I saved up for twenty years, and for our anniversary we went to Australia. We went snorkeling on the Great Barrier Reef. It is amazing! One moment you're snorkeling in a few feet of water, and you see the reef. Then, when you go over the edge, it's like going over a cliff. Literally you're looking down — I don't know — hundreds and hundreds, or even thousands of feet, into a bottomless abyss.

Nancy is normally a very adventurous person, but going over that edge and staring down at the abyss actually scared her. She wanted to get back into the boat. I said to her, "I've been saving up for twenty years for this trip. You will not get into the boat. You will swim over the abyss." She did not swim over the abyss. She got back into the boat.

For our thirtieth anniversary, we are going back to Wisconsin.

We used to have an argument about Lake Tahoe on the California-Nevada border. For years Nancy insisted that it was so deep that its depth could not be measured. I argued for the other side. One night we revisited this subject with great passion at a concert where the person sitting next to us happened to be an oceanographer. He interrupted us to tell us that in fact Lake Tahoe's depth had been measured to the precise foot. It was a wonderful moment.

But the soul has yet to be measured.

For much of our lives, we live in the shallows. Then something happens — a crisis, a birth, a death — and we get this glimpse of tremendous depth. My soul becomes shallow when my interests and thoughts go no further than myself. A person should be deep because life itself is deep. A deep soul has the capacity to understand and empathize deeply with other people — not just himself. A deep soul notices and questions and doesn't just go through the motions. A deep soul lives in conscious awareness of eternity, not simply today. It notices and observes and reflects in surprising ways — we talk about a person of "hidden depths."

A soul especially has depth when it is connected to God. His eternal existence, omniscience, and love are all beyond measure.

> My soul is downcast within me;
>> therefore I will remember you....
> Deep calls to deep
>> in the roar of your waterfalls.

To speak about depth means that there is more going on than what we see on the surface. To love deeply or care deeply or value deeply means we have devoted time and effort and thought. To suffer deeply means to be wounded at the soul level. "Depth" is an expression of spiritual vastness.

In fact, one word in the Bible to describe an eternity without God is called in the Greek *abussos*. We get our word *abyss* from that. The soul without God for eternity is in an abyss. There is a depth to you that words cannot describe. In the great book of suffering, Job says, "I will speak out ... in the bitterness of my soul" — from the depth of his being.

This notion of depth is part of why the Bible speaks of the "soul of God." Many people don't know this, but there are more than twenty passages in the Bible that talk about *God's* soul. God says to his people, "I will make my dwelling among you, and my soul will not reject you. I will also walk among you and be your God, and you shall be my people." Everything God is stands behind this promise: "My soul will not reject you."

When Jesus was baptized, we are told, "A voice from heaven said, 'This is my Son, whom I love; with him, my soul is well pleased.'" God is speaking from the deepest place of his being.

The world conspires against our souls by blinding us to the depth and glory of their God-given design and tempting us to be satisfied with immediate gratification.

In high school, Steve was a wonderful football player. Hurting his knee in junior college, he dropped out, got married, and had a child. He never chose to defy God. He just drifted. It was easier to drink beer than work on his marriage, so he got divorced. It was easier to complain than to work with all his soul, so he lost his job. It was easier to avoid people who would challenge him to tend to his soul, so he hung out with people who would honor his desire for comfort above all. He lives with his son now. After being estranged for years, he is there only because he has nowhere else to go. He watches vast amounts of porn in his bedroom to pass the time. He has lost his health. He does not even take care of his body. He is waiting to die, and when he does, no one will mourn.

But outside Steve's bedroom door, if he only knew, his son waits for him to say one word of sorrow, or regret, or love. It takes a little, such a tiny little depth in the soil to give the seed a chance. The shallow soul is closer to being saved than it knows.

The Cluttered Soul. Some seeds fall among thorns, which grow up and choke the plants. Jesus said that is the condition where the worries of this life and the deceitfulness of wealth and the desire for other things come and choke the soul.

Somebody said a long time ago that if the Devil can't make you sin, he will make you busy, because either way your soul will shrivel. Our world will divert your soul's attention because it is a cluttered world. And clutter is maybe the most dangerous result, because it's so subtle.

Once a Yuppie came to see Jesus. He believed in God, he led a respectable life, and he wanted to make sure he had covered all the bases. Jesus told him he was doing real well. The Yuppie was just about to walk away when Jesus mentioned, casually, that there was just one more small detail to be taken care of: "Go liquidate your assets, write out a check giving the whole enchilada to World Vision, then come and hang with me, and you will find that your soul has been saved."

The busy soul gets attached to the wrong things, because the soul is sticky. The Velcro of the soul is what Jesus calls "desire." It could be desire for money, or it could simply be desire for "other things."

We mistake our clutter for life. If we cease to be busy, do we matter? A person preoccupied with externals—success, reputation, ceaseless activity, lifestyle, office gossip—may be dead internally and not even recognize it. And our world has lots of "other things."

You can get them from infomercials; you can buy them online; you can collect them in your garage and put them in your will.

It takes a little, such a tiny little uncluttered space to give the seed some room to grow. The cluttered soul is closer to being saved than it knows.

YOUR SOUL IS WAITING

I bought my final can of bean-and-ballpark soup not long ago. When I was in high school, I made a friend—a soul friend—and during my first time at his house, his mom made lunch for us with bean-and-ballpark soup. It became a kind of sacramental meal for us; it was as bad as it sounds.

The mother's name was Betty, and she lived to be ninety years old. She never did anything extraordinary. She just raised four children. She just held her family together as her husband wrestled with manic-depressive disorder decade after decade, before there was medication, not knowing what she would come home to each day. She lived in the same small house in Rockford, Illinois, her whole life. She never traveled. She never bought an expensive dress or an upscale car.

When she died, the chapel was packed. It was filled with lives that she had touched. It turns out that her house on Carolina Avenue, like that other house in Box Canyon, was one of the strange, small, unmarked outposts of a great soul. I brought a can of bean-and-ballpark soup with me to the funeral as a kind of final Last Supper to honor her soul.

A soul can be saved. But it will take softness and depth and space. The world won't help much.

I have been waiting.

I am shy—terribly shy—even in the most boisterous person. I can only whisper, never shout. You may never even notice me.

But I am here, waiting.

I do not lie on the surface. If you look and listen, patiently, you will know.

I speak through your confusion, through your wanting, through your hurt. When you stammer, when you say what you did not mean to say, it was I. When you watch a sunset, or hear a child laugh, or listen to a piece of music that causes you to suddenly become choked up, it is I that causes your eye to fill. When you are addicted, it is I that is chained.

When the sun burns up and the universe melts away, I will be here. Like Glenn Close in the movie Fatal Attraction, *I will not be ignored. I can be wounded, lost, repulsed, or redeemed. Your circumstances actually matter far less to your happiness than you think. It is my health that makes your life heaven or hell.*

I am your soul. I am here.

CHAPTER 4

LOST SOULS

I had grown up thinking I knew what a lost soul was, but now I was not so sure. Dallas said, "A ruined soul is a *lost* soul." What is a lost soul? Just someone God is mad at? When is a person lost? Is anyone lost today?

I had always thought that a lost soul referred to the soul's *destination*, not its *condition*. But it's the condition that is the real problem. If a car no longer works, it doesn't matter much whether it ends up in a junkyard or the valet parking section of the Ritz-Carlton. We are not lost because we are going to wind up in the wrong place. We are going to wind up in the wrong place because we are lost.

We live on the planet of lost souls.

The soul integrates the will and mind and body. Sin disintegrates them. In sin, my appetite for lust or anger or superiority dominates my will. My will, which was made to rule my body, becomes enslaved to what my body wants. When I flatter other people, I learn to use my mouth and my face to conceal my true thoughts and intentions. This always requires energy: I am disintegrating my body from my mind. I hate, but I can't admit it even to myself, so I must distort my perception of reality to rationalize my hatred: I disintegrate my thoughts from the reality.

Sin ultimately makes long-term gratitude or friendship or meaning impossible. Sin eventually destroys my capacity even for enjoyment, let alone meaning. It distorts my perceptions, alienates my relationships, inflames my desires, and enslaves my will.

This is what it means to lose your soul. It is not a cosmic threat. It is a clinical diagnosis. It is not "I could end up *there*." It is "I could become *that*." If you are a lost soul, your surroundings don't matter—I mean this literally—one damn bit.

THE DANCE WITH SIN AND THE SOUL

I suppose that the person I have sinned against the most is my wife. She was the first really serious girlfriend I ever had. I had been on many first dates, a fair number of second dates, a few third dates, but no fourth dates until hers.

The biggest difference between our maturity levels is that I thought I was far more mature than I was. I had never been in love before, but I had great confidence that when it happened, I would know. I had asked that question many times: "How do you know when you're in love?" The answer I always got—the answer I wanted to believe—was "You know." Actually, it was "You just know," said with a smile and a knowing nod.

With Nancy I just knew. Except for when I didn't. Except for when she did something that bothered me, something that didn't fit perfectly with my idealized, romanticized notion of what it would mean to have the greatest relationship ever.

When she would do something I didn't like—when she disagreed too vehemently or I felt as if she was getting too directive—I would feel something turn cold inside of me. I would distance myself from her by making less eye contact and touching her less and speaking a little coldly. On the night of our rehearsal dinner, which was supposed to be all music and magic, she did or said something that I did not like (and that I no longer have any memory of), but I remember with great clarity sitting in the car with her late into the night. In tears, Nancy said, "If you don't want to marry me, say so."

Love, anger, withdrawal, coldness, pain, guilt, melting. All this at a level too deep for my knowing. I had to keep two incompatible thoughts in my mind: "I am a good person" and "I want to inflict pain." So I had to separate them from each other; I had to disintegrate my mind. This pattern became so embedded that my will couldn't stop it.

We honeymooned in Wisconsin. A few days into our marriage, she moved toward me romantically, but I withdrew behind a book. I would intimate to her that I did not want sex, even though really I always wanted sex. But I knew my coldness would hurt her a little. My sin crept into my sex life.

Sometimes if we were with other people and she said something I didn't like, I would get a little distant and polite with her and make a little more eye contact and grow a little warmer toward whomever we were with. My mind was conflicted with thoughts of love and thoughts of bitterness; my feelings were split between intimacy and coldness. My will would move away from her in anger until things got really bad and she cried and I would feel guilty and move back toward her. My face and the tone of my voice could create the effect on her that I wanted without ever being totally open about the deeper recesses of my mind and will. Sin was in my anger. Sin was in my deception. Sin was in my body—the way I would use my face to both conceal and to hurt.

Nancy wanted us to see a counselor. We did for a few times that first summer, but I did so quite grudgingly. And then no more after that, not for many years. I had a doctorate in clinical psychology because I believed other people needed help, but not me. Sin was in my pride. Sin was in my stubbornness.

Marriage is revealing. If only I had eyes to see the sin in just about every area of my life.... This dance of withdrawal and approach continued on-and-off for fifteen years. It was not the only dynamic in our marriage; we genuinely loved and enjoyed each other. But withdrawal was always at least beneath the surface, hibernating until the next painful episode.

And then it got much worse. I had been colder longer and meaner than maybe ever before. Nancy got back from a two-week trip, but I still did not thaw. I remember picking her up at the airport and still being politely distant; I can remember our eight-year-old daughter at the airport trying to push the two of us together for a hug. She knew that we were pushing apart. Children always know more than we think.

That night Nancy told me that she could not do the dance anymore. She wasn't going anywhere. But this dynamic was not about her. It was trouble inside of me, and I would have to work it out somehow. This began a year of anxiety and depression, of counseling and journaling, of little steps and painful talks and looking at the ugliness inside myself that I had never known was there.

The lost soul that I had gone into ministry to save was my own.

The lost soul that I had gone into ministry to save was my own.

I called Dallas and flew back to Box Canyon. We went for a long walk and a long drive. I tried to describe what was happening with Nancy and what I was learning about my own need to be seen — and to see myself — as someone other than who I really was. Dallas's wife, Jane, joined us for a while; she works as a counselor and a spiritual director. She drew a little diagram that I have to this day, illustrating how certain people view themselves as either the inflated superior being or the worthless empty person no one could love.

I began to feel my deep lostness.

As I unburdened myself to Dallas, I began to understand another soul truth: Confession really *is* good for the soul. The soul is healed by confession. Sin splits the self. It split me. It meant I tried to pretend in front of Nancy; I tried to pretend before the church that I was a better husband than I was. Sin divided my will; I wanted closeness, yet I wanted to inflict pain when I felt hurt.

As long as I keep pretending, my soul keeps dying. Oddly enough, I don't just pretend in front of other people. I pretend with God. My friend Scotty says that sometimes we ask for forgiveness, but we know full well we will go back to the same sin tomorrow. We don't really want forgiveness; we just want to get out of trouble. He says it would be better to pray like this: "Dear God, I sinned yesterday, I sinned again today, and I'm planning to go out and do the same sin tomorrow. In Jesus' name, Amen."

It may not quite reflect the maturity of "Thy will be done," but it is better to be an honest mess before God than a dishonest "saint." "You desire truth in the innermost parts," the psalmist said to God, and that's soul-talk. This is part of the sheer healing power of AA — Alcoholics Anonymous. Confession is good for the soul.

At the end of the day, Dallas and I prayed together. I prayed for forgiveness and healing. Dallas did something no one had ever done for me; as we prayed, he placed one hand on my chest over my heart. He asked God to bring wholeness to my soul. It felt to me about as close as I have ever felt to someone actually touching my soul. Finally, I began to move toward being whole. It is a source of joy to be able to say that. But even so, I struggle. I have other sins with Nancy. Then there are the sins that stand against me as a parent. And there are my sins as a friend, a pastor, a neighbor, a son, a consumer, and a global citizen.

As I had realized before at the conference full of twenty-somethings, I sensed now for myself that the soul searches for a father.

DISCONNECTED FROM GOD

The apostle Peter says, "There are sinful desires inside you, and they wage war against your soul." Your soul is what integrates, what connects, what binds together your will, then your mind (those thoughts, feelings, and desires going on all the time), and then your body (with all of its appetites, habits, and behavior). God designed us so that our choices, our thoughts and desires, and our behavior would be in perfect harmony with each other and would be powered by an unbroken connection with God, in perfect harmony with him and with all of his creation. That is a well-ordered soul.

The soul is what connects all those innermost parts together, connects them with God, and was made for harmony all the way through. Notice how the psalmist writes, "Bless the LORD, O my soul: and *all that is within me*." In other words, it is my soul that connects "all that is within me" and that cries out for integration, for wholeness, for oneness, for harmony. This can only happen when my soul — my whole life — is connected with God.

This is precisely why when somebody asked Jesus once, "What is the most important of all the commandments?" he answered, "Love the Lord your God with all your heart, and with all your soul, and with all your mind, and with all your strength." It is not coincidental that all the parts of the person we have been talking about are here in the most important commandment. Your heart (that is, your will, your choices), your mind (all your thoughts and desires), your strength (all of your body), and your soul are all to be bound together and focused on love of God, and then the love of all that flows out of this.

What sin does is break this connection, with God and his love, and it disintegrates one's life. That's why the basic human problem is at the soul level. James uses a really interesting word — twice. In James 1:8 he says, "A double-minded man is unstable in all his ways" (KJV). Then later he repeats, "Wash your hands, you sinners, and purify your hearts, you double-minded." The word translated "double-minded" in the New International Version is the Greek word *dipsuchos*. *Psuche* is the Greek word for soul, and literally it could be translated "you double-souled," "you split-souled," or "you fractured soul." Sin fractures and shatters the soul.

Even though we don't talk much about the soul, our language reflects this in such deep, often unconscious ways. People will say things such as "I feel like my life is falling apart" or "I just can't seem to get myself together. I just can't seem to get my act together. I seem to be going to pieces. I am coming apart at the seams." These are the cries of a soul that was made to be whole. As Parker Palmer puts it, "The divided life is a wounded life, and the soul keeps calling us to heal the wound."

The heart is primarily the seat of the choices we make from the core of who we are. So the picture here is a person who does what is right, sometimes, but is torn by the desire to do otherwise. Perhaps it means I avoid outright adultery but allow myself other forms of sexual gratification that dishonor my spouse. Or I avoid stealing, but I never live with openhanded generosity. I have my foot on the accelerator and the brake at the same time.

When my will is consistently, freely, joyfully aligned with what I most deeply value, my soul finds rest. That is wholeness. When I live with half-hearted devotion, my soul is always strained.

When my will is consistently, freely, joyfully aligned with what I most deeply value, my soul finds rest. That is wholeness. When I live with half-hearted devotion, my soul is always strained.

God's intent is that my will would be able to oversee, or direct, my mind and then my body. So if everything is working right, if you are as God created you to be, then your body will be the obedient, easy servant of your mind and your will, what you choose. Your mind also will think about and feel those things you direct it to.

My will exists to be surrendered to God in every way. My mind should be under the control of my will. If that were the case, I would simply be able to choose life-giving, truthful thoughts and healthy desires. In turn, my body would always submit to my mind. My habits would line up with my values. My appetites would be governed by rational thought.

But too often the will lacks the power to control the mind, allowing it to go places we don't want to go. Our bodies are these collections of appetites that veer out of control and habits that drag us down paths we don't want to travel. I am having lunch with a friend, and one of us orders dessert even though the person knows he should not have ordered dessert. To make matters worse, when the dessert is served, it is huge. It is on this gigantic plate. There is whipped cream all over the place, embarrassing the eater. It makes that guy appear to have a huge appetite for sweets. Then a solution to his embarrassment appears. The plate is so large that the huge dessert might seem small by comparison. The next sentence to come from the guy who ordered it?

"Big plate. Little dessert."

Now, where did that sentence come from? It came from the

mind. What is the mind doing? The body said, "I want something. I want dessert. I want fat and sugar and all that stuff that's not good for me." The will said, "Okay, fine with me. Go for it, buddy." That leaves the mind with a problem: "I want to think of myself as a person of self-control and strong will, and yet here I am indulging in something I know is not going to be good for me. And I also don't want my friend to think of me as gluttonous or unhealthy." The mind could go back to the will and say, "Hey, will, don't do this. You don't need all those calories and fat. Besides, your friend will think you have no self-control." But the will is not going to do that. The will has already said yes to the body, so what does the mind have to do? The mind has to find some way to rationalize the decision the will has made so that the mind can continue to feel good about the kind of person he is. Does any part of this sound familiar?

Thus, out of the thousands of things the mind could notice, it focuses its attention on the ratio of the dessert volume to the surface space of plate, which is actually larger than is the case for desserts in many restaurants. The mind says, "Now, what this means is that if I only look at the dessert, I am an out-of-control pig. I can't deal with that." So the mind goes straight to the obvious deception: Big plate, but little dessert.

All this happens way faster than we can consciously process. Then the mind continues, "Not only is that thought true, but if I could get the mouth to express that thought out loud, then it can help the other person realize I am someone with greater self-control than dessert size alone might indicate." So not only can I rationalize what my will is doing, but I can also control the thoughts that others are having about me. All that in four little words: "Big plate. Little dessert."

I won't mention which of us ordered the dessert, because the sanctity of confidentiality between priest and penitent is absolute.

That may seem like a trivial example, but behind it are all the dynamics that make jealousy, lust, greed, anger, abuse, and deceit possible. We find ourselves, because of sin, in this odd place where we want to do good things, but we don't. We go to church, we read

the Bible, and we think about God as a God of love. The fruit of
the Spirit is love and joy, and we say, "Yeah, that's what I love." But
when we look at our lives, the real problem isn't just the stuff we
see; it's the thousands of things we don't. "Big plate. Little dessert."
This is the human condition.

Paul says, "For in my inner being [in my mind and even in my
spirit] I delight in God's law." I'm pro-love. I'm pro-joy. I'm pro-
truth. Who isn't? "But I see another law at work in me ..." — that
is, the members of my body. The habits that my eyes, my hands,
and my mouth violate all the time. They violate way, way, way
more than I'm aware of. "... waging war against the law of my
mind and making me a prisoner of the law of sin at work within
me" — my body.

Jesus made this diagnosis a long time ago when talking about
temptation. "The spirit" — notice the language again — "is willing,
but the flesh [the body] is weak." This is
very true and largely ignored and forgotten in our day. Habits eat willpower for
breakfast. So there is the will, there is
the mind, and there is the body. They are
working badly, sometimes in ways that are kind of humorous to us,
but often in ways that are horrible and unspeakably tragic.

*Habits eat willpower
for breakfast.*

Sin is the sickness that our souls have inherited.

CHAPTER 5

SIN AND
THE SOUL

Fake sunglasses can damage your soul.

Researchers at Duke, North Carolina, and Harvard universities have all examined the impact of "fake adornment" on our ethics. In one study a group of women was given expensive Chloé sunglasses to wear, but half of them were told the glasses were cheap knockoffs. Even though they were assigned at random, the knockoff group was more than twice as likely to both cheat and steal in a subsequent study than women who believed they were wearing the real deal. In another study, people who thought they were wearing fake sunglasses were more cynical in their attitudes toward other people. We fake it in life to bolster our ego. But the result is, we feel like phonies and become more deceptive and cynical with others—so exquisitely sensitive is the need of the soul to be whole.

How do I come to grips with the truth about my own soul? Why is it so evasive? Why can I often see other people more clearly than myself? Soul language has to involve sin language. Why? Because sin disintegrates, obliterates, wholeness. Your soul cannot function properly if sin is present.

Sin is not just the wrong stuff we do; it's the good we don't do. It's the starving children we don't want to look at, the volunteering we avoid, the poor we don't want to serve, and the money we don't want to give. How can good church folk turn their backs on the people Jesus called "the least of these"? Diversion and collusion. First, we remind ourselves that we haven't committed the really bad sins such as bank robbery or serial murder. Then we make a pact with each other: I won't call you on it if you won't call me on it. I have been told by religious book publishers that no one will buy books about feeding the hungry or clothing the naked. Collusion is pretty widespread.

No Little Sins

Unlike our legal system, sins are not weighted by their seriousness. There are no misdemeanors in the realm of sin. Sin is sin, and it is serious because of what it does to the soul. The apostle Paul wrote, "Here is a trustworthy saying that deserves full acceptance: Christ Jesus came into the world to save sinners—of whom I am the worst." Why does Paul say he is the worst? The late John Stott wrote, "Paul is not saying he did a careful study of every sinner in human history and found out he came in last place. The truth is, rather, when we are convicted by the Holy Spirit, an immediate result is we give up all such comparisons." Paul was so vividly aware of his own sins that he could not conceive that anybody could be worse.

This is the language of every sinner whose conscience has been awakened and disturbed by the Holy Spirit. There is real neurological evidence for the power of spiritual reflection to make us aware of our sin. Christians actually use a different part of their brain to self-evaluate than non-Christians. In a study conducted in Beijing, researchers compared which part of the brain people used to evaluate both themselves and others.

The study is summarized in an article with the snappy title, "Neural Consequences of Religious Belief on Self-Referential Processing." Non-religious subjects used one part of the brain (the ventral medial prefrontal cortex, in case you're interested) to evaluate themselves, but another part (the dorsal medial prefrontal cortex) to evaluate others. Christians used the same part of the brain to evaluate themselves that they used to evaluate others. Researchers hypothesized this is because they were actually using a kind of "Jesus reference point" for self-evaluation; they were really asking, "What does God think of me?" UCLA researcher Jeff Schwartz said that this study is one of the most important scientific papers published in the last decade. Prayer, meditation, and confession actually have the power to rewire the brain in a way that can make us less self-referential and more aware of how God sees us. But these impediments to sin may not come easily.

> *Prayer, meditation, and confession actually have the power to rewire the brain in a way that can make us less self-referential and more aware of how God sees us.*

Peter wrote, "Dear friends, I urge you, as foreigners and exiles, to abstain from sinful desires, which wage war against your soul." In our day, soul language often conjures up images of herbal-tea-drinking, Birkenstock-wearing, flower-growing, scented-candle-lighting, conflict-avoiding granola crunchers. But that's not what Paul is talking about when he talks about soul work. He says soul work is war. Spiritual war.

People in certain church circles attribute just about every inconvenience to spiritual warfare. Once, on the way to a speaking engagement, I barely made it on time because I had a flat tire. One of the people at the site where I was speaking said, "Boy, that's spiritual warfare." Well, maybe, but I found myself wondering, "If a demon really was trying to keep me from getting to that church on time, why wouldn't it mess with the transmission or the fan belt or the ignition system? A flat tire is the only thing I know how to fix in a car." Peter was not talking about the ordinary consequences of life, but the soul-destroying effects of disintegration.

Sin's ability to disintegrate the soul is the subject of a book by a Duke professor named Dan Ariely. In *The Honest Truth about Dishonesty: How We Lie to Everyone — Especially Ourselves*, Ariely is astounded by how widespread people's tendency is to cheat, be self-centered, lie, and be deceitful. He discovered that we are driven by two primary motivations. One, we want to receive selfish gain. We want to avoid pain. We want it so much that we are willing to lie or cheat or deceive for it. We want what we want, and we're willing to cheat to get it. Two, we want to be able to look in the mirror and think well of ourselves. That means we all want to view ourselves as basically good, honest, honorable people. Clearly these two motivations are in conflict with each other.

How can we enable our selfishness with deceit on the one hand but at the same time view ourselves as honest, wonderful, noble people? "This is where our amazing cognitive flexibility comes into play. Thanks to this human skill, as long as we cheat only a little bit, we can benefit from cheating for selfish gain and still view ourselves as marvelous human beings." What Ariely calls our amazing cognitive flexibility, the apostle Paul calls "the godlessness and wickedness of people, who suppress the truth by their wickedness."

It took me longer to read Ariely's book than I expected because someone stole the book from me, and I had to get a new copy. Who would steal a book about being dishonest? When they read it, what did they think about this book about dishonest people who would cheat and lie and steal?

Ariely's book clearly gives empirical verification for what you and I know happens all the time. Here is a tiny example I hope you cannot relate to: Ariely says, "Over the course of many years of teaching, I have noticed that there typically seems to be a rash of deaths among students' relatives at the end of the semester. It happens mostly in the week before final exams and before papers are due." Guess which relative most often dies? Grandma. I am not making this stuff up.

Mike Adams, a professor at Eastern Connecticut State University, has done research on this. He has shown that grandmothers are ten times more likely to die before a midterm and nineteen times more likely to die before a final exam. Worse, grandmothers of students who are not doing well in class are at even higher risk. Students who are failing are fifty times more likely to lose Grandma than nonfailing students. It turns out that the greatest predictor of mortality among senior citizens in our day ends up being their grandchildren's GPAs. The moral of all this is, if you are a grandparent, do not let your grandchild go to college. It'll kill you, especially if he or she is intellectually challenged.

SIN BEGETS SIN

Ariely goes on to write about how a single act of dishonesty is not a petty act, because it ends up shaping how we view ourselves. We are souls. Everything is connected. That singular deceit determines how far we will allow our standards to slip and still regard ourselves as basically good people. Every act of wrongdoing (sin) leads to the greater likelihood of another act. Start as small as you want. Stand in the express lane in the grocery store with too many groceries in your cart—seventeen grocery items in the twelve-or-less aisle. Try to board a plane when it's not yet your group's turn. "I'm not dishonest. I'm in a hurry. I'm too important to wait my turn." Something as small as a pair of fake sunglasses will still register on the scale of your soul.

Once you rationalize that first sin, it makes it more likely that you will say, "It was the traffic," when it wasn't the traffic. It makes it more likely that you will say, "I'm sure I sent that email," when you know you did not send that email. If you say it often enough, you will come to remember and believe you sent that email. It makes it more likely that you will cheat on an expense account or fudge your résumé. Is it any wonder that workplaces become filled with gossipy, cynical, judgmental people exaggerating their own contributions and minimizing those of others? We tolerate jealousy, sabotage, and greed, but only enough so we can all feel good about ourselves—because we're good people.

Sometimes wrongdoing increases so much it can't be rationalized anymore. When that happens, the common response is not repentance. It is not people saying, "Oh God, how could this happen? How could I be capable of this?" What happens is much more like what happens when you are on a diet. If you cheat moderately for a while, you will think you're still on the diet. But if somebody blows it a lot, what will often happen is that their mind will say, "Well, I've already blown it, so I might as well just binge and eat anything I want to."

When I cross over that line where I can't pretend anymore, generally what will happen is that moral behavior will collapse completely. You see this sometimes in scandal-ridden companies or corrupt executives, in abusive families, in the nightmare of child molestation. Even in the unbelievably scarring words hurled at anyone who does not look or think like us. You reach a point where you know that what you are doing is so wrong, but you don't care anymore. You see it in whole cultures: Rwanda. North Korea. Stalin's Russia. The Third Reich.

Do you know what the name of this effect is in psychological research? It's called the "What-the-Hell" effect. I can't pretend anymore, so I might as well just wholly give in to my urges and gratify what I want, regardless of the consequences. What might those consequences be? What the hell? That dynamic is present not just in those bad companies, those high-profile executives, and those horrible regimes. It is right here. In me. In you. What the hell?

The soul is able to bear only so much truth. Perhaps it's like having a child: if anyone really knew the cost ahead of time, no one would ever do it. In the same way, if I were to see the depth of my own self-deceit and self-centeredness, I might give up on the possibility of change before I start. But there is hope, for as Francis Fenelon reminds us, "God is merciful, showing us our true hideousness only in proportion to the courage he gives us to bear the sight." And the prophet Jeremiah bears witness: "I remember my affliction ... the bitterness and the gall. I well remember them, and my soul is downcast within me." The soul remembers things that I forget.

I saw my advisor from psychology graduate school recently. He reminded me of a time when I had done an internship and received a fairly negative evaluation. I had no memory of what he was talking about.

He reminded me in some detail—and with a little too much enjoyment. Yet nothing registered in my brain. He still had the file in which my deficiencies had been pointed out. There was my name.

Oh, yeah! I realized, as he spoke, that it was no coincidence that I had simply forgotten (or, more accurately, "put it out of my mind"). A negative evaluation did not fit with the positive achieving image I wanted to have of myself. So I did the reasonable thing and found a way to forget reality so that I could maintain the image. There was another alternative, of course. I could have stepped back from my feelings, open to looking at reality.

My soul was trying to tell me something: "Don't be a therapist!" I might have saved lots of time and money if I had been willing to pay attention. But it was too threatening to my sense of worth. So I forgot it for twenty-five years until remembering that it wouldn't cost me anything anymore. On the other hand, when my mind focuses on that which is good, the integrating power of the soul calls to my will to choose it, and my body to live it.

Yet another experiment offers insights into the soul. This one involved 450 students at UCLA. Researchers divided them into two groups and asked one group to remember some trivial memory: ten books you had been assigned to read in high school. They asked the other group to try to remember the Ten Commandments. The students in the ten books memory group engaged in typical widespread cheating. The students in the Ten Commandments group did not cheat at all. Merely the act of trying to remember the Ten Commandments made them think, "I was made for something better." This despite the fact that not a single student in the Ten Commandments group was able to recall all of the commandments.

> "The law of the LORD is perfect, refreshing the soul." That doesn't mean moral rules can transform a human being, but it does mean the soul was made to love and do the will of God.

"The law of the LORD is perfect, refreshing the soul." That doesn't mean moral rules can transform a human being, but it does mean the soul was made to love and do the will of God.

A GOD-GIVEN ACHE FOR GOODNESS

Conviction is not just the pain of getting caught or pain over consequences. It means a God-given, really sober sense of remorse over what I ought to feel remorseful about. It's a God-given ache for goodness.

A prodigal son comes to his senses. The mighty King David is humbled by a phrase: "thou art the man." A sinful woman aching for forgiveness bathes Jesus' feet with her tears. In the same way the stomach hungers for food, the conscience hungers to be cleansed. It is a God-given ache for goodness.

During the most painful era of our marriage, I would often look at a picture of our children. There's an old prayer that goes, "God, help me to be the man my dog thinks I am." I don't even think the dog was too impressed with me then. But when I looked at our children, it somehow reminded me of the man I wanted to be. Somehow, looking at their faces made me see both the soul that I was and the one I wanted to be. It made me ache to be a better person.

I sat with Dallas and Jane during a visit that was painful, but there was hope in the pain. There is a pain that means things are coming apart. But then, sometimes there is a pain that means that things might be able to come back together. Surgery can be as painful as stabbing, but it leads to healing. I knew I was beginning to heal.

I contrasted the pain that was bringing healing for me with that of a family I have known my whole life long, who had gone to church every week of their lives. Both parents died in their old age. It turns out the mom had been desperately unhappy, writing about how she wished so much she had married somebody else. At the same time, the father had been living a secret life. Nobody knew. Nobody found out until after he died, discovering pictures that revealed his deception. Their daughters were miserable. There had been this pattern of deceit and pain. So I held my pain dear, because it meant I was no longer deceiving myself. My soul was responding to its God-given ache for goodness.

I left Box Canyon those many years ago and flew home to talk with my wife. I felt like Humpty Dumpty, trying to put together what all the king's horses and men could not. But the soul will surprise you sometimes.

CHAPTER 6

IT'S THE NATURE OF THE SOUL TO NEED

In the 1991 comedy film *What about Bob?* Bill Murray plays the title character, a neurotic, phobic, obsessive-compulsive personality with innumerable needs. I quote (from memory): "Problems breathing. Problems swallowing. Numb lips. Fingernail sensitivity. Pelvic discomfort. What if my heart stops beating? What if I'm looking for a bathroom and I can't find one and my bladder explodes?" Richard Dreyfuss plays the exasperated, impatient therapist who is stuck caring for him.

Your soul is Bob. You are Richard Dreyfuss. It is the nature of the soul to need.

The will is a form of energy. You can drive and stretch and push the will. The mind has an endless ability to think and feel. You can direct your attention. You can focus and study. The body is your little power pack. You can place demands on your body. You can exercise it, strengthen it, hone it, and force it to run for miles.

But it is the nature of the soul to need.

The soul is a little like the king on a chessboard. The king is the most limited of chess pieces; it can only move one square at a time. But if you lose the king, game over. Your soul is vulnerable because it is needy. If you meet those needs with the wrong things, game over. Or at least, game not going well.

NEEDY MAN

A great scholar named Hans Walter Wolff wrote a classic study of how the Old Testament writers understood personhood. He said that the word *flesh* stands for humanity's bodily form with its mortality, physical strength, and limitations. *Ruah,* the Hebrew word for "spirit," speaks of human beings as they are empowered — human existence with breath and will and inspiration. Wolff's chapter on *nephesh* — the Hebrew word for "soul" — he titled "Needy Man." Another name for *nephesh* is Bob. Your soul is a needy man, a needy woman.

Thomas Aquinas wrote that this neediness of the soul is a pointer to God. We are limited in virtually every way: in our intelligence, our strength, our energy, our morality. There is only one area where human beings are unlimited. As Kent Dunnington puts it, "We are limited in every way but one: we have unlimited desire." We always want more: more time, more wisdom, more beauty, more funny YouTube videos. This is the soul crying out. We never have enough. The truth is, the soul's infinite capacity to desire is the mirror image of God's infinite capacity to give. What if the real reason we feel like we never have enough is that God is not yet finished giving? The unlimited neediness of the soul matches the unlimited grace of God.

Our soul's problem, however, is not its neediness; it's our fallenness. Our need was meant to point us to God. Instead, we fasten our minds and bodies and wills on other sources of ultimate devotion, which the Bible calls idolatry. Idolatry is the most serious sin in the Old Testament, leading one scholar to conclude that the primary principle of the Old Testament is the refutation of idolatry. Idolatry, according to author Timothy Keller, is the sin beneath the sin. Anytime I sin, I am allowing some competing desire to have higher priority than God and God's will for my life. That means that in that moment I have

We all commit idolatry every day. It is the sin of the soul meeting its needs with anything that distances it from God.

put something on a pedestal higher than God. That something is my idol. All sin involves idolatry.

We all commit idolatry every day. It is the sin of the soul meeting its needs with anything that distances it from God.

We have another problem. We often don't know what our souls are truly devoted to. Most people, especially religious people, would probably say their souls are devoted to God or a higher calling or an ideal. We want to believe that's true even as we devote our souls to something else. Consider as honestly as possible the following statements. If any of them even slightly resemble your thoughts, it is quite possible you have discovered the true devotion of your soul:

- I think about money a lot, as in getting more of it. Sometimes I fantasize about winning the lottery or coming into a big inheritance. I have a mental wish list of the things I'd like to buy if money were no object.

- I wish I had more power and control over others. It seems as if my spouse and kids just don't respect me enough. Ditto at work. I know I would handle it carefully — I would just like to be a more powerful person.

- I have missed important family events in order to pursue my career. I justify it by telling myself and my family that this is what it takes to provide for them. I tell myself that if I keep working hard, I will reach a level where I will be able to relax a little and spend more time with the people I love.

- I consider myself an honest person, someone with good values. But I would set those values aside to pursue something important to me if I knew no one else would know about it.

- I have desires that I prefer not to have my spouse know about. If I am confronted by any of those desires, I become defensive and try to justify it.

- I have secrets that I am willing to lie to protect.

- More than once I have had arguments over something I wanted to do but my spouse did not want to do. Or over something I wanted to buy that my spouse didn't think I should buy.

- Aside from my family and others I love, there are things in my life that if they were lost or destroyed, it would crush me, devastate me.

- If my doctor told me I had to give up (alcohol, cigarettes, red meat, salt/sodium, sugar, caffeine, etc.) because it was seriously putting my health at risk, I would find it difficult to the point of being impossible. I likely would not tell anyone in order to avoid accountability.

- If you asked my family what was most important to me, they would likely refer to my job, my favorite hobby, making money.... They would probably not say it was them.

- I love God, and I want to more closely follow him, but there is one thing that always seems to get in the way, and it's

    _____.

If your soul is devoted to something that becomes more important to you than God, that is your idol. The soul cannot give up its idol by sheer willpower. It is like an alcoholic trying to become sober by promising himself that he won't drink anymore. It never works. In many ways, what the Bible calls idolatry we call addiction. You can be an addict and never touch a drop of alcohol or a gram of cocaine. Nice things like food, shopping, recreation, hobbies, and pleasure can move imperceptibly from casual enjoyment to addiction. I know men who buy expensive boats and then feel compelled to be on the water every weekend, not so much because they enjoy "serial boating," but because if you're spending this much on something, you had better enjoy it. Idols always turn us away from our freedom.

This is where grace comes in. I cannot replace an idol by turning away from it. I must turn toward something.

This is where grace comes in. I cannot replace an idol by turning away from it. I must turn *toward* something.

As Timothy Keller puts it, "We are all governed by an Overwhelming Positive Passion." He gives an example: In the book of Genesis, a young man named Jacob meets a young woman named Rachel and tells her father he wants to marry her. He offers to work for Laban seven years if he can marry Rachel. Laban says yes. "So Jacob served seven years to get Rachel, but they seemed like only a few days to him because of his love for her." Jacob discovered time is relative way before Albert Einstein said anything about it. Every single day for seven years, Jacob doesn't just show up for work; he does so with a song in his heart. Why did seven years seem like a few days? Because he had an overwhelming positive passion, and that changes everything.

Zacchaeus had an overwhelming positive passion for money. As a tax collector for Rome, he gave up relationships, integrity, and honor for his idol.

Then one day he met Jesus.

"Today I'm repaying everyone I've cheated four times over, and I'm giving half the rest of my money to the poor," Zacchaeus said. What led him to do that? He had a new overwhelming positive passion.

The soul must orbit around something other than itself—something it can worship. It is the nature of the soul to need.

OVERCOME BY THE SOUL'S NEED

What the soul truly desires is God. We may try to fill that need with other things, but the soul will never be satisfied without God. The psalmist describes that need in terms of losing consciousness: "My soul yearns, even faints, for the courts of the LORD."

When I was a young associate pastor in my first church, the senior pastor (also named John) invited me to preach on Sunday morning. When it came time for the sermon, I stood at the pulpit, and five minutes into my sermon, I fainted dead away. The platform was made of marble, so I hit the ground hard, with a loud smack. After the service I apologized to John. I felt horrible because this was a Baptist church, not a charismatic church where you get credit for that sort of thing.

"I'll understand if you never ask me to preach again," I told him.

"Don't be ridiculous," he responded, and in a few weeks he asked me to preach again. And I fainted again.

I was certain that I was finished in that church, but he asked me to preach again the following week. He even mentioned he was having the marble floor covered with carpet to protect my fall, just in case.

"I'm going to have you keep preaching until you quit fainting or it kills you."

These many years later, I just received a letter from that church asking if I would preach for their seventy-fifth anniversary. John had long since retired, but the current pastor wrote, "People here still remember you ... I thought that was nice ... as the fainting preacher."

I don't think that was what the psalmist had in mind when he said his soul faints from yearning for God. I laugh whenever I recall those first attempts to preach, but it also offers a graphic reminder of my soul's deepest need. Fainting is a scary thing. My fainting said more about my nerves than my desire for God. I have often wondered what it must be like to want God so deeply that it leads you to faint.

There is another grace-filled memory about that church that still melts my soul. Through that church, I met a woman who attracted my attention. I had always thought if I ever did get married, it would be to a Midwestern girl. But then I met that California girl at this church. She was so beautiful, I never thought a woman who looked like that would ever even go out with me. And as a matter of fact, that particular woman never *did* go out with me.

But then I met Nancy through that church, and she was even more beautiful. She not only went out with me, but married me. We now have Californian children and a Californian dog and serve at a Californian church.

I am glad God has a sense of humor. It is good for the soul.

ACCEPT YOUR SOUL'S NEEDINESS

Sometimes when I talk to my soul, I call it "Bob" to remind myself to be patient with it. Bob's need for God is enormous, but that's okay. Bob's neediness only invites more of God's generosity. He's not going anywhere. Besides, oddly enough, the family kind of likes him.

Our soul begins to grow in God when we acknowledge our basic neediness.

> *Our soul begins to grow in God when we acknowledge our basic neediness.*

Francis Fenelon was a brilliant spiritual writer and successful cleric who stood up to King of France Louis XIV and allowed himself to be displaced as royal tutor. He lived disgraced in exile. But in obscurity and humiliation, his soul thrived. He understood the condition of his soul:

> In order to make your prayer more profitable, it would be well from the beginning to picture yourself as a poor, naked, miserable wretch, perishing of hunger, who knows but one man of whom he can ask or hope for help; or as a sick person, covered with sores and ready to die unless some pitiful physician will take him in hand and heal him. These are true pictures of our condition before God. Your soul is more bare of heavenly treasure than the poor beggar is of earthly possessions.... your soul is infinitely more sin-sick than that sore stricken patient, and God alone can heal you.

Good people — especially people of faith — do not like to think of themselves as "poor beggars" who are "sin-sick." We fill our soul's desires with everything that counters that image, trying to convince ourselves that everything is well with our souls. It isn't. Our souls faint and yearn and cry out for God.

How do we respond when we understand the neediness of our souls?

CHAPTER 7

THE SOUL NEEDS
A KEEPER

I and no one else am responsible for the condition of my soul.

In my early fifties I was given a sabbatical: seven weeks with nothing to do. The elders at our church invited me to take it. Actually, they insisted that I take it. I needed it because I was becoming increasingly frustrated and impatient and preoccupied. I felt as if I had too much to do and not enough time or ability to do it. I was obsessed with the external things that needed to be done around me. I was operating on the unspoken assumption that my inner world would be filled with life, peace, and joy once my external world was perfect. That's a great recipe for a healthy soul, as long as you live in a perfect world.

During my sabbatical, it was easy to "ruthlessly eliminate hurry from my life," as my friend and mentor Dallas Willard had so wisely counseled. I found myself thinking that I'm a better person when I'm on sabbatical than I am when I'm working for God at a church, and I knew that was just plain wrong. I began to form a new goal: I want to be as relaxed as I am on vacation while being as productive as I am at work.

There was only one place to learn about that. So I drove back to Box Canyon. I had a whole day to spend with Dallas. I told him that I felt frustrated because the people at the church I served were not changing more. I asked him what I needed to do to help our church experience greater levels of spiritual growth.

Long pause ... "You must arrange your days so that you are experiencing deep contentment, joy, and confidence in your everyday life with God."

Huh?

"No," I corrected him. "I wasn't asking about me. I was asking about other people. I was wondering what I need to make the church do. I was thinking about a book everyone should read, or a program everyone should go through, or a prayer system everyone should commit to."

> *You must arrange your days so that you are experiencing deep contentment, joy, and confidence in your everyday life with God.*
> **DALLAS WILLARD**

"Yes, Brother John," he said with great patience and care. "I know you were thinking of those things. But that's not what they need most. The main thing you will give your congregation — just like the main thing you will give to God — is the person you become. If your soul is unhealthy, you can't help anybody. You don't send a doctor with pneumonia to care for patients with immune disorders. You, and nobody else, are responsible for the well-being of your own soul."

"I'm trying," I said. "I learned long ago about the importance of having a quiet time when I read the Bible and do daily devotions; I do my best to start each day that way."

"I didn't say anything about having a quiet time," he gently corrected again. "People in churches — including pastors — have been crushed with guilt over their failure at having a regular quiet time or daily devotions. And then, even when they do, they find it does not actually lead to a healthy soul. Your problem is not the first fifteen minutes of the day. It's the next twenty-three hours and forty-five minutes. You must arrange your days so that you are experiencing total contentment, joy, and confidence in your everyday life with God."

"But how can I have total contentment, joy, and confidence?" I responded. "My work isn't going nearly well enough. Lots of people are not happy with me. I am inadequate as a pastor, husband, and father. Every week I carry the burden of delivering a sermon and knowing I'll have to feel the pain if it doesn't go well."

"I didn't say you should experience total contentment, joy, and confidence in the remarkable adequacy of your competence or the amazingly successful circumstances of your life. It's total contentment, joy, and confidence in your everyday experience of God. This alone is what makes a soul healthy. This is not your wife's job. It's not your elder's job. It's not your children's job. It's not your friend's job. It's your job."

The stream is your soul. And you are the keeper.

THE LAW OF CONSEQUENCES

This is the message of one of the most important and challenging chapters in the Bible. The ancient practice of holding children guilty for parents' misdeeds left confusion about the whole idea of responsibility for the soul. The Word of the Lord came to the prophet Ezekiel:

> What do you people mean by quoting this proverb about the land of Israel: "The fathers eat sour grapes, and the children's teeth are set on edge"? As surely as I live, declares the Sovereign LORD, you will no longer quote this proverb in Israel. For every living soul belongs to me, the father as well as the son — both alike belong to me. The soul who sins is the one who will die.

Then God lays out a few long case studies to illustrate his meaning, and in case anyone missed it, he repeats it again: "The soul that sins is the soul that shall die."

This is what we might call Reality 101 when it comes to the soul. It is the law of consequences. Paul put it like this: "You reap what you sow." Even people who have never read the Bible or gone to church can recite that verse, even though they probably have no idea where it comes from. Mostly we like to say that as a warning to other people. Apparently we believe that by some magic, the law of consequences doesn't apply to us.

- I can spend without getting into debt.
- I can lie without getting caught.
- I can let my temper fly without damaging my relational life.
- I can have a bad attitude at work and get away with it.
- I can avoid disciplining my children without their getting spoiled.
- I can neglect the Bible and still know God.

Our capacity to live in denial about the law of consequences is huge and is damaging to the soul. In the Bible it takes God a long time to teach the human race about this. One of the ways he tries to teach this concept is in an obscure and really bizarre little story that starts the book of Judges.

As the book begins, Israel is fighting: "It was [at Bezek] that they found Adoni-Bezek and fought against him, putting to rout the Canaanites and the Perizzites. Adoni-Bezek fled, but they chased him and caught him, and cut off his thumbs and big toes."

I'm not making this up.

When I grew up in Sunday school, our main educational technology was called the flannel graph. I don't ever remember seeing this character named Adoni-Bezek with no thumbs, no big toes. Seems like a gory way to start off a book in the Bible. As I've learned from years of reading and studying and teaching the Bible, there's always a good reason for whatever is in the Bible. In this case, if you learn about this story, it can actually save you a world of pain.

Adoni-Bezek said, "Seventy kings with their thumbs and big toes cut off have picked up scraps under my table. Now God has paid me back for what I did to them."

Things were violent back then, but even then this was big-time torture. Adoni-Bezek does thumb and toe removal not once, but seventy times. It was his signature move. Then, to intensify the humiliation of these rival kings, he feeds them by having them eat scraps under the table.

He was sowing terror and cruelty and getting away with it.

Until one day . . .

Now *he's* the ex-king with no thumbs and no toes under the table. But notice—he doesn't say, "Israel did this to me"; he says, "As I have done, so God has repaid me." All those years, all that torture, all those victims—someone was watching the whole time. It's not just that there is a Law of Consequences in the universe. There is a God of Justice in the universe. "Do not be deceived: God cannot be mocked. A man reaps what he sows." And the primary arena in which this is true is that little plot of ground that has been assigned to your care—your soul. A soul that is not kept properly will surely die.

Keep Your Soul by Speaking to It

The formation of the soul is the most important process in the universe. John Keats wrote, "Call this world if you please 'The vale of soul-making.'" In our day, we talk a lot about self-talk. Books get written about the importance of self-talk. Apparently, that's a really important part of the human condition. Everybody here talks to themselves. In the Bible, people talk to their souls. The difference between talking to yourself and talking to your soul is that the soul exists in the presence of God. So you will see in the Psalms and elsewhere people speaking to their souls because when you speak to the soul, it naturally turns to prayer because in the soul God is always present.

Your soul is not the same thing as your emotions. We live in a world where we're encouraged to think that our feelings dominate our lives and that we are powerless over them. But even contemporary research indicates the power God has placed in the soul to be master of our emotions. In one study, researchers presented subjects with pictures of angry faces. Half of the participants were told simply to observe the faces. The other half were instructed to label the emotion on each face. The simple act of labeling the emotion reduced its emotional impact on their own moods. It also reduced the activation of the brain region associated with strong primitive emotion.

Normally when we are angry about something, we mutter under our breath: "Well, that sure was stupid, you big dummy." We beat up on ourselves or, worse, on others. We may find temporary relief from that, but the soul still cries for attention. The next time you blow something—when you're frightened, when you're dissatisfied—instead of mindless self-talk, speak to your soul: "Why are you afraid, O my soul?" At first it might seem a little silly, but remember, you are the keeper of your soul. Only you.

When I speak to my soul, "Why are you angry, O my soul?" it actually changes my brain.

Not long ago I got really angry at somebody. Finally I literally stopped in my tracks because I was so immersed in anger and said, "Soul, why are you so angry?" Something interesting happened. I found that I just began to pray, and it was like God saying to me, "John, you are not your anger." It's like my soul had a place to stand with God, and we could talk sensibly about my anger, even as it ebbed from my soul.

"I am the master of my fate: I am the captain of my soul."

No, I am its keeper, not its captain. I did not make it, and I cannot save it from death.

That's why soul-care is a different task than self-care. I do not care for my soul only for my own sake. It is only mine on loan, and it is coming due soon.

The psalmist wrote that blessed people are like trees planted by rivers of water, which yield their fruit in season, and whose leaves do not wither; they prosper in all they do. In the ancient Middle East, trees were rare. Rain was scarce. Deserts were plentiful. But if a tree were planted by a river, it was no longer dependent on uncertain weather or the surface conditions of the soil. It could flourish at all times because its roots allowed the water to stream into each part of the tree to bring it life. You couldn't see the roots, but no one could miss the green leaves or fresh fruit.

Just as in the little parable that started this book, our soul is like an inner stream of water that gives strength, direction, and harmony to every other area of life.

WHAT'S BLOCKING THE STREAM?

Once there were two brothers who could not get along. They had grown up together, played together, fought together, laughed together; perhaps they had been close.

But when they grew up and their parents died, they had an argument about how to divvy up the estate. It grew severe enough that they couldn't get along anymore; the money was more important than the love of one brother for another.

One of them—the younger, who didn't have any leverage—decided to get some outside help. He approached a rabbi: "Teacher, tell my brother to divide the inheritance with me."

That teacher was Jesus, but he didn't play arbiter; instead, he gave a warning and told a story. The warning was that a person's life does not consist in the abundance of their possessions. The story was about a wealthy farmer who harvested a bumper crop one year. He said to his soul, "Soul, you have many goods laid up for many years to come; take your ease, eat, drink and be merry." His life became an upscale village filled with expensive homes. But God said to him, "You fool! This very night your soul is required of you." When Jesus says the man's soul will be *required*, he uses language from the business world; it's a term that would describe a loan that had fallen due. Our souls are on loan to us. One day, God will review with us what our souls have become. That is what will matter from our lives.

The stream is your soul. For it to flow freely, the keeper of the stream must clear it of anything that becomes more important than God.

Instead of a humble village being fed by a life-giving stream, that farmer's life had become an upscale village filled with expensive homes. That cries out for my attention. I will be happy if I have more money. I will be happy if I have this moment of sexual gratification. I will be happy if I can upgrade to a cooler car. I will be happy if I can win more applause. I will be happy if the stock market is kind to my IRA. I am drawn to whatever is shiny and bright and new in the village.

We will always take the most care of that which we value most deeply.

DENTED CARS, DENTED SOULS

I drive an old Honda; it's been dinged up enough times that I don't often notice a new ding. One day I pulled out of a parking space in a very crowded parking lot, and I heard this sound of metal scraping metal. It was not a loud sound, so I hoped that meant there was no damage to the other car. I got out of the car and saw a tiny scratch on the car I had just barely touched. It wasn't a dent. It wasn't a crumple. Just a little scratch — something I would ignore if it were my car. But this was not my car. It belonged to someone else. And unlike my car, it was not a beater. It was an Italian car.

Rhymes with Terrari.

Everything but my soul told me to take a quick glance around the parking lot to see if anyone saw what had happened and then quickly get into my little Honda and put some distance between me and the car with an imperceptible scratch.

My soul told me I had to leave a note.

Later that day, the owner called me back. He appreciated my leaving a note but was committed to having his car restored to its original condition. A car of such worth should not be driven in such a degraded condition. Do you know how much it costs to restore perfection to a Ferrari?

We exchanged several phone calls back and forth, all quite gracious, but each one meaning more bad news for me. Then I got one last call from the owner of perfection: "I've decided to get a new car, so you don't owe me anything."

I wanted to call him back and ask him if I could have his ruined car, but I decided not to push my luck.

Even a Ferrari is only a ding waiting to happen.

We live in a world that teaches us to be more concerned with the condition of our cars, or our careers, or our portfolios than the condition of our souls. Maybe because a dent in a soul is more easily concealed than a dented car. Maybe because a dented soul is harder to fix. After a while, the dents pile up, and they stop bothering us. We hardly notice. One dent more isn't going to make much difference.

I am responsible to take care of my soul not just for my own sake. The condition of my soul will affect the people around me, just as when my body is sick it can infect others who get too close.

The keeper of your soul is responsible for its dents. You are the keeper of your soul.

One scholar put it like this: "Both for his own sake and for the sake of the community every Israelite must take good care of his own soul." If he fails to do this at crucial points, the soul is to be cut off. Repeatedly in the book of Leviticus, Israel is told that if people do not properly observe the Sabbath, or Passover, or if they profane what is holy, or despise the commandments, ". . . such persons must be cut off from their people." That may seem harsh, but an unhealthy soul is like a cancer in the community. I care for my soul because if it becomes unhealthy, it will infect others. You have seen it happen. Someone comes to the office in a foul mood and it casts its spell on everyone.

I have done slightly better caring for my soul than I have caring for the many animals that have come into my life. We have had a long history of pets in our family that did not go well. One of the first times I drove up to the church in Menlo Park where I now serve, it was from southern California. We had just gotten our first goldfish, and fish don't travel well. Goldfish especially don't travel well. That goldfish gave its life for this church. A little later we got a little bird for our daughter Mallory, and she called it Jo-Jo.

We were on vacation one time. Nancy and I came back early. Our kids were still with the grandparents, and neighbors had watched Jo-Jo for us. They gave the bird back to us, and we had it for a day or so, when finally Nancy said to me, "I don't think that's Jo-Jo." I said to Nancy, "You think our neighbors killed our bird, got a replacement, gave us the fake, and then lied to cover it up? You really think that is what happened?"

That's actually what happened.

It gets better (or worse). We had to tell Mallory that Jo-Jo was dead, and, naturally, she was devastated. She insisted on a burial, but this happened when we lived in Chicago and the ground was frozen. We had to wait until the ground thawed, which would not occur for another six months. So for six months poor little Jo-Jo rested in the freezer, and every time we opened the freezer, we were reminded of the consequences of deceit.

I keep my soul carefully because I want to bring life and not death to those around me.

YOUR SOUL IS FOREVER

Jesus said, "Do not be afraid of those who kill the body ... rather, be afraid of the One who can destroy both soul and body in hell." A lot of people would be shocked to know Jesus said something like this because we think of him as always saying comforting words, especially "Fear not." I have not counted them, but I have been told that there are more than 365 "fear nots" in the Bible. So why all of a sudden is he telling us to be afraid? Because the stakes are so high—the body eventually ages and wears out, but the soul lives forever. And how you live determines the destination of your soul. We don't like to think about this, but the Bible teaches that we will one day stand before God who is the judge of our eternal destiny. If you live your life in deliberate violation of his will and his ways, your soul will eventually be destroyed by being completely separated from God. That was the essence of Jesus' warning: Protect your soul. Guard it. Make room in your life to care for it.

I went to Box Canyon to seek ways to improve my church. I left with a greater understanding of the needs of my soul—that I had little to offer the people of my church if I was not tending to those needs, not just for fifteen minutes every morning, but all day. Every day. I wrote Dallas's words on a piece of paper, and they hang above my office door: "Arrange your days so that you experience total contentment, joy, and confidence in your everyday life with God." They are the first words I see every morning when I come to work. *The stream is your soul. And you are the Keeper.*

CHAPTER 8

THE SOUL NEEDS A CENTER

On an overcast day in Florida in the late winter of 2013, a man whose family had lived in the same home for generations suddenly lost his life when a sinkhole opened up beneath the home's foundation, causing the floor to collapse and simply swallow up the house. Experts say that in parts of Florida, the limestone that lies beneath the earth's surface is slowly being dissolved by acidic rainwater. When enough rock is eaten away, the void simply collapses under the weight of what an inadequate foundation can no longer support.

Gordon MacDonald once wrote about how what he called the "sinkhole syndrome" happens in a human life. It may be triggered by a failure at work, a severed relationship, harsh criticism from a parent, or for no apparent reason at all. But it feels like the earth has given way.

It turns out, MacDonald wrote, that in a sense we have two worlds to manage: an outer world of career and possessions and social networks; and an inner world that is more spiritual in nature, where values are selected and character is formed—a place where worship and confession and humility can be practiced.

Because our outer worlds are visible and measurable and expandable, they are easier to deal with. They demand our attention. "The result is that our private world is often cheated, neglected because it does not shout quite so loudly. It can be effectively ignored for large periods of time before it gives way to a sinkhole-like cave-in." He quotes the haunting words of Oscar Wilde: "I was no longer captain of my own soul." The sinkhole, says MacDonald, is the picture of spiritual vulnerability in our day.

WHEN THE SOUL LACKS A CENTER

As I mentioned earlier, the New Testament book of James uses a fascinating word to describe this condition. It's often translated "double-minded," but the Greek word is *dipsuchos* — we might think of it as double-souled, or split-souled, or the un-centered soul. Here are a few of the indicators when a soul lacks a center.

A soul without a center has difficulty making a decision. One of the pictures James uses of this condition is that the double-souled person is like a wave on the sea, driven forward one moment and backward the next. People whose souls are rooted in a center find it brings clarity to their decisions. Steve Jobs, who was surely single-minded in his purpose, was said to always wear the same outfit every day (blue jeans, black turtleneck) because that way he did not have to waste energy making an unimportant decision. John the Baptist had a different wardrobe but the same one-option approach to fashion.

A classic counter to this in Scripture is the character of Pontius Pilate. He struggles with the decision of what to do with Jesus. He tries to talk Jesus into saying what will allow Pilate to free him. He pesters the religious leaders without making the decision that his authority would have allowed. He asks the crowd to let him off the hook, but they opt for Barabbas. When the soul is not centered, one is never sure what temptations are worth resisting or what sacrifices are worth making.

A soul without a center feels constantly vulnerable to people or circumstances. When David is running from Absalom, he becomes completely exhausted and stops to rest. The literal translation of the text is to "re-soul" himself. It is Elijah's soul that grows terrified under the threat of Jezebel. He runs and hides. Meanwhile, God treats all his "parts." God gives his body a rest and some food; he allows Elijah's mind to hear his still small voice; he appeals to Elijah's will to return to the battle. Eventually Elijah's soul is restored, but only because he found his center.

The disconnected soul lives in vulnerability. When one of our daughters was three years old, she loved to play a little game we called "kitty in the nest." After bath time, when it was time to dry her off, she would pretend she was the kitty. She would sit in front of me on the floor and make sure my legs made a kind of rectangle around her (that was the nest). It was very important that my feet touch each other, because that meant there was no open space where anything could sneak in to hurt the kitty. If I let my feet separate, she would physically move them together while shaking her head and saying, "Kitty in the nest, Daddy, kitty in the nest!" I thought about explaining to her that if there ever *was* a kitty in the nest it would not be a safe place for the birds, but I thought that might spoil the game.

A soul without a center lacks patience. In the book of Numbers, when the people grew impatient with God's long journey through the wilderness, the text says that "their souls grew short." The same usage occurs in the book of Judges; Samson's soul has no center because he simply rambles from the pursuit of power to pleasure to women to revenge; the nagging of one single woman is enough to make this powerful man "grow short in soul." On the other hand, the character of the proverbially patient Job is said to be "long-souled."

King Saul was a big man with a short soul. When he was to lead Israel against their enemies the Philistines, he grew impatient waiting for the prophet Samuel to show up at Gilgal to offer sacrifices. His solution was to take matters into his own hands and offer the sacrifice himself. The result was a shattered covenant with God and a giant step in the disintegration of his soul.

> *The soul craves to be safe. We cannot stop the craving nor provide the safety. But there is a nest: "Have mercy on me, my God ... for in you I take refuge. I will take refuge in the shadow of your wings...."*

When I am with my children in a line at the grocery store, or in the car on a crowded freeway, my soul does not have to be tapping its toes and drumming its fingernails. If I am always in a hurry to be somewhere else, it's an indicator that my soul has not yet found its home. "Nothing in man seems so intent upon God as the soul.... The soul seeks the Mighty One as though he is the soul's own home, as though it can only be at home with him.... The soul is hidden in God's creating hand: 'In his hand is the *soul* of every living thing'" (Job 12:10).

The soul without a center is easily thrown. We were with friends recently at kind of an open-air street fair, and at one spot there was a mechanical bull that tries to buck people off. We stopped to watch, but nobody would climb on the thing and give it a try. The man operating the bull said, "Watching isn't nearly as fun as riding. Who's going to be the one to get on the bull?" So somebody in my little group said to me, "Why don't you go?" I never took the rodeo class when I was in seminary, but nobody else would go, and I wanted to see something.

So I told the remote-control-bull operator that I wanted to ride. He took one look at my middle-aged body and asked, "Are you sure?" That pretty much guaranteed that I would not back down.

"There are twelve levels of difficulty on this bull," he explained. "It might not be all that easy, but the key is you have to stay centered, and the only way to do that is to sit loose. People try to clamp on too tight. Don't do that. You have to be flexible. If you think you can be in control of the ride you'll never make it. You have to follow the bull. You have to keep moving. Shift your center of gravity as the bull moves."

I got on the bull and it started slow, and then it started moving faster and jostling around, and I was holding on real tight. Then I remembered his advice, so I loosened up, and it kept moving faster and jolting and bucking and jumping. I was hanging on sideways. My arms were flailing around all over the place. I just hung on and finally the bull slowed down and it stopped, and I was still on the bull. It wasn't pretty but I made it. I imagined how surprised the operator of the bull would be that I had triumphed. I looked over at the man who was operating the bull, and he looked over at me. Shaking his head, he smiled and said, "That was level one."

Level two lasted maybe a second. The bull won.

Sometimes life comes at us at level one. Level one is kind of like Mayberry in the 1960s sitcom. It just shuffles along without major complications. Level one is the week after your honeymoon when nothing is more exciting or complicated than finding a place to store the three blenders you got as wedding gifts.

Life never stays at level one.

It gets complicated. Stuff happens. Opie turns out to have a major anxiety disorder. An addiction that has hibernated for two decades suddenly wakes up. My job is threatened. My faith is riddled with doubts. My friend betrays me. I can't sleep. My health becomes uncertain. If your soul lacks a center when life comes at you fast, you will be thrown off the bull. No matter how hard you try to hold on, eventually you'll get thrown.

The soul without a center finds its identity in externals. My temptation when my soul is not centered in God is to try to control my life. In the Bible this is spoken of in terms of the lifting up of one's soul. The prophet Habakkuk said that the opposite of living in faithful dependence on God is to lift your soul up in pride. The psalmist says that the person who can live in God's presence is the one who has not lifted their soul up to an idol.

When my soul is not centered in God, I define myself by my accomplishments, or my physical appearance, or my title, or my important friends. When I lose these, I lose my identity.

HOLD ME, DADDY

A soul without a center is like a house built over a sinkhole. "How collapsed you are my *soul,* and how you sigh over me." On the other hand, the soul comes alive when it is centered on God. "Let the morning bring me word of your unfailing love ... for to you I lift up my soul." A friend once told me how his three-year-old son, who is now a grown man in his thirties, used to approach him when he was tired or frightened or just needed to be held. The little guy would reach out with his arms and say, "Hodja, Daddy. Hodja," his three-year-old version of "Hold me, Daddy." Years later, my friend recalled, his son came home from work and discovered his wife had left him for another man. He was devastated and called his dad and asked if he could come over. Of course he could, so he drove the five hours to his parents' home, walked in the door, and collapsed into his father's arms. My friend told me, "I could almost hear him crying, 'Hodja, Daddy. Hodja.'"

When we reach out to God, we are lifting our souls up to be nurtured and healed. A soul centered in God always knows it has a heavenly Father who will hold its pain, its fear, its anxiety. This is spiritual life: to place the soul each moment in the presence and care of God. "My soul cleaves to you, your right hand upholds me."

It is much harder than it sounds to keep our souls centered on God. We hold on tightly, but often to the wrong things. But staying centered on God — his word, his ways — is the essence of life for the soul.

Thomas Kelly wrote,

> We feel honestly the pull of many obligations and try to fulfill them all. And we are unhappy, uneasy, strained, oppressed, and fearful we shall be shallow. . . . We have hints that there is a way of life vastly richer and deeper than all this hurried existence, a life of unhurried serenity and peace and power. If only we could slip over into that Center! . . . We have seen and known some people who have found this deep Center of living, where the fretful calls of life are integrated, where No as well as Yes can be said with confidence.

"My soul clings to You; your right hand upholds me." When God seems distant, "My soul thirsts for God, for the living God. When can I go and meet with God?" Brother Lawrence called this "practicing the presence" of God, and the most important part of that practice lay in "renouncing, once and for all, whatever does not lead to God."

A very simple way to guard your soul is to ask yourself, "Will this situation block my soul's connection to God?" As I begin living this question I find how little power the world has over my soul. What if I don't get a promotion, or my boss doesn't like me, or I have financial problems, or I have a bad hair day? Yes, these may cause disappointment, but do they have any power over my

It's not about perfection. It's not about adequacy. It's not about your competence.... It's about holding on to God, because the soul was made to be connected with him.

soul? Can they nudge my soul from its center, which is the very heart of God? When you think about it that way, you realize that external circumstances cannot keep you from being with God. If anything, they draw you closer to him.

ENEMIES OF THE SOUL

There are two main enemies that lead to a soul disconnected from its center. One is sin. Sin cannot coexist with a soul centered on God. If I choose to live in bitterness, or to indulge lust, or to deceive my wife, I am choosing to keep God out of my thoughts. Conversely, when I center my soul on God, I am less likely to sin. I'm not likely to speed if I see a squad car; I'm not likely to play video games at work if my boss is watching; I'm not likely to sin while God is present to my mind. It is not just that God is always watching and always knows the condition of our hearts; it's our knowing that he is there.

The other disconnect is what might be called the "troublesome thought." This soul-enemy is actually much more pervasive. It's not necessarily a sin. It's simply a way of thinking that does not take God into account. The troublesome thought begins with any normal concern you might have. For example, you open your quarterly statement from your 401K and notice that instead of gaining, your fund lost a few hundred dollars. Certainly reason to be concerned, but then you begin a succession of thoughts that practically consume you: Will I have enough to retire? What if the next quarter posts another loss? Should I pull my money out of this fund? By entertaining these thoughts, you are allowing something to squeeze God out of your life. It's one thing to pay attention to your retirement account, but when you leave God out of the equation, your soul loses its connection.

I do this all the time. I get disappointed about how a talk went—and then have a series of thoughts about how I'm not being successful enough and am therefore not leading well enough, not serving my people well enough. Or I sit down at my desk and am so overwhelmed at all that needs to be done that I fixate on how hard I'm going to have to work, how I may have to work through lunch, how it seems like all I do is work.

A soul disconnected from its center is like an unplugged computer. It is like a fish left on the banks of a river that would give it life. Eventually it crashes. It dies.

The soul cannot be centered without God.

CHAPTER 9

THE SOUL NEEDS A FUTURE

Other creatures can live happily for today and not think about tomorrow. But not us. Our blessing and our curse is our ability to extend ourselves into tomorrow. "There's no future in it" is the main reason people give for leaving a relationship, or a job, or a home. We cannot help this about ourselves. "In the day of my trouble ... my *soul* refused to be comforted," says the psalmist.

The soul needs a future.

This is a problem, because we are not just souls, we are enfleshed souls, and we know what happens to flesh.

A prophet named Isaiah made an observation to the people of Israel thousands of years ago when they were suffering under an oppressor named Babylon.

A voice of one saying, "Cry!"
One said, "What shall I cry?"
All flesh is like grass, and all its glory is like the flower of the field.
The grass withers, the flower fades ...
But the word of our God stands forever.

A voice (God) says, "Isaiah, tell people: 'All flesh is like grass, all human glory is like the flower of the field.'"
Temporary. Disposable.

This is true whether you believe the Bible or not.

As a young lady, Violet Asquith met Winston Churchill at a dinner party, where he ignored her most of the evening. When he finally turned to her, it was to ask her an unexpected question: "How old are you?" "Nineteen," she said. "And I," said Churchill despairingly, "am thirty-two already. Older than anyone else who counts, though." He then launched into an impromptu commentary on Isaiah's observation: "Curse our mortality! Curse ruthless time. How cruelly short is the allotted span for all we must cram into it. We are worms, all worms."

And then, with Churchillian confidence in his own transcendent uniqueness, "But I do believe I am a glowworm."

No human being—not even Churchill—can out-glow mortality. In fact, the whole point of this text is, don't put your hope in human ingenuity.

*No human being—
not even Churchill—
can out-glow
mortality. In fact,
the whole point of
this text is, don't put
your hope in human
ingenuity.*

When Isaiah spoke, people living in the wealth and power and ambition of Babylon *knew* the glory of Babylon would last forever. It did not. Babylon is long gone. Of course—we're different. We're smarter than Babylon. We have technology.

All flesh is as the grass: you don't have to believe in the Bible. Just look around. The fastest athlete in track will eventually be defeated by arthritis. The most beautiful supermodel in the world will not be on the cover of *Sports Illustrated* Swimsuit Issue when she's ninety-seven years old. Even wealthy, powerful CEOs get betrayed by their bodies and die.

This is not a popular truth. I thought one time at the church where I work I would help people remember it by developing a new liturgy where I would say: "Your flesh is like the grass"; and the people would respond: "We are grass indeed." It didn't go over so well.

ETERNITY IN OUR HEARTS

The soul needs a future.

This is so because there's another truth about the human condition: "[God] has also set eternity in the human heart." This is where we're different than grass: The grass doesn't know it's here today, gone tomorrow.

There is a cave in New Zealand where they have literal glowworms; the inside of the cave is lit up by thousands of these phosphorescent little creatures. They spend most of their lives as larvae. When they finally hatch and get their wings, they have no mouths, no way to feed—they only live for one single day. They have one day to fly, explore career opportunities, attract a mate, get married, have children, and then die.

On the other extreme, guess how old the oldest living thing in the world is? It's called Posidonia Oceanica—a clump of Mediterranean seagrass. Scientists date it at one hundred thousand years old. When Isaiah said those words, this living thing had already been alive for more than ninety millennia.

All flesh is as the grass. Life spans can range from a day to a hundred thousand years. Yet all these living things will die, and it doesn't bother them at all. They don't need a future.

We are different. We have a radar for eternity. Human beings have an instinct that life does not end with the grave. And we have a hunger this world cannot satisfy. Again, you don't have to believe in the Bible to see this. Look at the pyramids. Visit a nursing home.

God has placed eternity in the human heart.

The Bible says the reason God has done that is that we were made for an eternal existence with him. And the most important thing we are doing in this life is preparing for the life that is going to come.

My old boss from Chicago, Bill Hybels, was studying the Bible for a sermon in a restaurant one time. A young woman looked over and asked, "Why are you reading *that*?"

Bill looked back and said (this is an exact quote): "Because I don't feel like going to hell when I die." Bill has a little problem expressing himself assertively sometimes.

She retorted, "There is no such thing as heaven or hell."

Bill thought, *This is gonna be interesting.* He turned. "Why do you say that?"

She said, "Everybody knows that when you die, your candle goes out ... *poof!*"

"You mean to tell me there's no afterlife?"

"No."

"So that means you must be able to just live as you please?"

"That's right."

"Like there's no judgment day or anything?"

"Right."

Bill continued, "Well, that's fascinating to me. Where did you hear that?"

She said, "I read it somewhere."

"Can you give me the name of the book?"

"I don't recall."

"Can you give me the name of the author of the book?"

"I forgot his name."

"Did that author write any other books?"

"I don't know."

"Is it possible that your author changed his mind two years after he wrote this particular book, and then wrote another one that said there is a heaven and a hell? Is that possible?"

"It's possible, but not likely."

Bill: "All right, let me get this straight. You are rolling the dice on your eternity predicated on what someone you don't even know wrote in a book you can't even recall the title of. Have I got that straight?"

She looked back. "That's right."

Bill summarized, "You know what I think, my friend? I think you have merely created a belief that guarantees the continuation of your unencumbered lifestyle. I think you made it up, because it is very discomforting to think of a heaven. It is a very discomforting thought to think of a hell. It is very unnerving to face a holy God in the day of reckoning. I think you made it all up."

The conversation got a little edgy after that.

God has put eternity into your heart. Every one of us has those moments when we hear it. When our first child was born, the very first moment of her life, I took her from her mom and held her in my arms. Something happened that I did not expect and had never experienced: It was like I could see a whole span of a life in an instant. I said to Nancy, "This little strand of red hair will turn gray and then white; this soft rosy skin will grow wrinkled and mottled; this pliable little body will grow bent with age. She will grow old, and then we'll die and be gone, and then she'll die and be gone."

Nancy said, "Let me hold the baby. You're gonna creep her out."

Dallas Willard puts it like this: You are an unceasing spiritual being with an eternal destiny in God's great universe. He used to encourage me to write this down and read it out loud as a reminder of my true identity:

> *I am an unceasing spiritual being with an eternal destiny in God's great universe. But I'm also like grass. I'm going to die.*

God did not plant death in the human heart. Death came because of sin. That includes my sin. Human self-sufficiency can't get me out of this one. If I don't have a hope that is eternal, I don't have a real hope at all. But God made a way.

Isaiah said, "All flesh is like grass ..., but the word of our God stands forever."

The gospel of John says that one day — "The Word became flesh."

The Word is one of the titles that John uses for Jesus. The Word here means Jesus, the Son of God, the expression of God, the incarnation of God.

The Word — which is eternal — became flesh. And all flesh is as the grass. Which is temporary. Disposable. Dies.

Jesus humbled himself. Jesus took on the very nature of a servant. Jesus lived among the poor. He washed feet.

He was struck and would not strike back. He was hated, and he loved back. He was condemned, and he forgave back.

In Jesus, the Word became flesh. They whipped him 'til he bled; they put him on a cross; they hung him 'til he died; they laid him in a tomb, and they sealed it with a stone.

All flesh is as the grass.

But God will do anything to keep the soul alive. The psalmist speaks about God rescuing the soul from the jaws of death, allowing it to escape the sword and doom, delivering it from the threshold of destruction. "In whose hand is the *soul* of every living thing."

Pain Comes, Then Joy

The soul needs a future. God planted eternity in our hearts so that we would not stop seeking life beyond ourselves. Jesus tried to speak of this to his disciples not long before he died: "In a little while you will see me no more, and then after a little while you will see me."

Their confusion is so great they pester him with questions, and he tries again:

> A woman giving birth to a child has pain because her time has come; but when her baby is born she forgets the anguish because of her joy that a child is born into the world. So with you: Now is your time of grief, but I will see you again and you will rejoice, and no one will take away your joy. In that day you will no longer ask me anything.

A woman giving birth to a child has pain; but when her baby is born she forgets the pain....

Really?

When our first child was born, we went through a class called Lamaze. In those days they would not use the word *pain*, because "pain" sounds like kind of a downer. They said the mother-to-be might experience some "discomfort." Husbands were to be "coaches"; I was to coach Nancy so that she didn't have pain. Coaching mostly consisted of telling Nancy to breathe. The goal was to use no drugs or pain medication, just cleansing breaths. It wasn't clear to me how my telling Nancy to breathe—which she had been doing pretty much her whole life—would prevent pain when an object the size of a bowling ball was coming out of her body.

Nancy was in labor twelve hours. They had to give her Pitocin several times, which made it much more intense. The baby was turned the wrong way so that the hardest part of her skull pressed against the most tender part of Nancy's spine—I remember the nurse said the baby was "sunny-side up," which sounded cheery to me, but didn't perk Nancy up at all.

For eleven hours I massaged her lower spine with a tennis ball and encouraged her to breathe. I was bent over; my back was aching; my hands were sore; I never complained. She will never know what I went through to have that baby.

The worst moment came when the doctor reached inside my wife's body and physically wrenched the baby 180 degrees. Nancy let out a yell I will never forget. I was the coach, and I knew I had to do something. "Nancy, are you experiencing some discomfort?"

She actually still remembers that.

Jesus' point is not that a woman can't bring the pain to memory. His point is that the joy of giving life outweighs the pain of giving birth. What starts in pain, ends in joy.

The disciples say, "What does he mean? What does all this 'in a little while' stuff mean?"

Jesus says, "I will tell you. Here's how it is in this world now that I have come . . ."

To paraphrase a line from a movie: There will be great pain, and there will be great joy. In the end, joy wins. So if joy has not yet won, it is not yet the end.

Jesus is crucified. The pain is overwhelming—not the end.

Jesus is risen—the joy is overwhelming.

This characterized the church. Followers of Jesus were beaten and rejoiced; they were put in prison and sang songs; they lived in poverty and were joyfully generous.

Jesus was right—no one could take away their joy.

The soul needs a future, like Winston Churchill's wonderful glowworm comment. He lived maybe the most remarkable life of the twentieth century. But all flesh is as the grass.

He died.

They held his funeral in St. Paul's Cathedral. When it was done, a bugler went up in the Dome of St. Paul and played "Taps," the tune that signifies that the day is done, that darkness has fallen. Time for sleep.

Everyone thought that was the end.

When the last note died out, on the other side of the dome, another bugler played "Reveille" — time to get up; time to get up; time to get up. We know where his hope lay.

In his "In a little while" speech to his disciples, Jesus made a promise that's so wonderful it's hard to believe. It has to do with question-asking.

The disciples were always pestering Jesus with questions: "Hey Jesus, can I sit at your right hand? Hey Jesus, how many times do I have to forgive this guy? Hey Jesus, why was this man blind from birth? Hey Jesus, what's this parable mean? Hey Jesus, shall we call down fire from heaven to blast the Samaritans? Hey Jesus, what do you mean in a little while?"

When we had a child, we were totally unprepared for the constant barrage of questions. Why? Why? Why? One time in the car, when Laura was about two, I decided to turn the tables. I suddenly bombarded her with questions: "Hey Laura, why is grass green? Hey Laura, why is the sky blue? What makes the car go? Where do babies come from?" Laura looked terribly confused; her lower lip began to tremble. Nancy, who had to handle the questions full-time from Laura every day, was thrilled that the shoe was on the other foot. "Keep going," she said to me. "Make her cry!"

I wonder if Jesus ever got tired of all the questions.

Underneath them all was the great question of every human heart: Why? We all have this one great question: Hey Jesus, why does a little boy have a brain tumor? Hey Jesus, why do hungry children keep dying and wars keep breaking out? Hey Jesus, why did my child run away? Why did my marriage fall apart? Why did my father suffer from a crippling depression?

Jesus said one day: In a little while — I'll be gone. Things won't be right. You will see terrible things: Illness. Hunger. Injustice. Sexual depravity. Massive deceit. Corruption in high places.

Then, in a little while — it will seem like a long time to you, but in eternity it's only a little while — I'm coming back. I will set it all right. Joy wins.

Indeed. "In that day you will no longer ask me anything."

That's the promise.

The soul needs a future.

> "It is the nature of joy that all questions grow silent, and nothing needs explaining." We will see the goodness of God. The world will be re-born. Pain will be defeated. There will be no more questions.

CHAPTER 10

THE SOUL NEEDS
TO BE WITH GOD

If you read through the Bible, you get the sense that the soul was designed to search for God. The Hebrew Scriptures—which might be thought of as the Great Soul-Book of human literature—are almost obsessed with this thought. The soul thirsts for the Mighty One (Ps. 63:1). It thirsts for him like parched land thirsts for water (Ps. 143:6). Like a laser it focuses the full intensity of its desire on him (Ps. 33:20). It lifts itself up to him (Ps. 25:1), it blesses him (Ps. 103:1–2, 22), it clings to him (Ps. 63:8), and it waits for him in silence (Ps. 62:1). "Indeed, the soul lives in God." The soul seeks God with its whole being. Because it is desperate to be whole, the soul is God-smitten and God-crazy and God-obsessed. My mind may be obsessed with idols; my will may be enslaved to habits; my body may be consumed with appetites. But my soul will never find rest until it rests in God.

In the beginning when God created the world, he planted a garden in the east, in Eden. The garden gets described at some length in the Bible. God made all kinds of trees grow out of the ground that were pleasing to the eye, many bearing fruit sweet and good. He decorated the garden with flowers and put fish in the streams, birds in the sky. Eden was the perfect home God created for his greatest creation: man and woman, Adam and Eve. God made the whole earth so that he would have a place to be *with* man and woman, you and me. The garden God created represents God's great desire for "being with."

For the soul to be well, it needs to be with God.

One of the most intriguing phrases in the Bible is where Adam and Eve "... heard the sound of the LORD God as he was walking in the garden in the cool of the day." God is Spirit, which means he doesn't have a body, legs, or feet. What does it sound like when God goes for a walk?

The point of this remarkable phrase is that walking is something you do with somebody you care about—a friend with a friend, a child with a parent. Two people in love would go for a walk. It's not really about the walk; it's about being with someone. This God—this God of the Bible—is a God who wants to "be with." Our souls were made to walk with God.

But the man and the woman sin, deliberately hiding from God among the trees of the garden. Yet God would not be denied. He went after them—in fact, the whole narrative of the Bible is all about God going after us. Relentlessly pursuing us. As Adam and Eve hid behind the trees God created, he called out, "Where are you?" Physically, he knew exactly where they were. What God was really asking was, "Where are you in relation to me?" All God has ever wanted is to be with you, with me. How can that happen?

A VERY BRIEF HISTORY OF LIFE WITH GOD

Consider the biblical character Enoch. We know hardly anything about him, but we're told Enoch walked with God. Noah walked with God. God was with Abraham, his son Isaac, and his other son Ishmael. God was even with Jacob, a manipulative deceiver. Then a whole tribe, the nation of Israel.

God was also with Joseph—and here's where "with God" starts to get interesting. Joseph ran into a really hard stretch in his life, and we learn that "the LORD was with Joseph" in slavery, and then, in prison. In other words, God is not just in the garden anymore—he shows up even in the most painful and difficult places. That's good news for anyone in trouble, and a hint of the Good News to come.

Then God is with Moses, Gideon, Samuel, Ruth, David, and many others until one day God cuts a hole in the wall, and a baby is born. We're told, "and they will call him Immanuel (which means, 'God with us')." Now in Jesus we get a little glimpse of what this "with God" life is like. Not just that, Jesus makes this staggering claim in John 15: "I am the vine; you are the branches. If you remain in me and I in you, you will bear much fruit; apart from me you can do nothing." I am the vine; you are the branch.

Bearing fruit means that we will do wonderful things in our lives for God and his kingdom, but we don't really have to try all that hard. Instead, we are to make sure we are "with God." That's what it means to "abide in the vine" — live intimately with Jesus from one moment to the next. "If you don't do that," Jesus says, "nothing much will come out of your life." It's kind of like he invites his followers into an experiment because they're just very ordinary people. How much can an ordinary person do in life on this earth with God in the ordinary moments? And how can I really make sure my soul is with God all the time?

Jesus offers us what he described in John 3:16 as "eternal life." Just about anyone who has attended church, and even people watching NFL football on Sundays, have heard of John 3:16. Those who think about eternal life usually think the phrase refers to immortality — a life that never ends. Technically, they are right, but the way it is used in the New Testament is not only about duration. It's not about quantity of years but quality of life with God.

Jesus began this grand experiment with his twelve followers. They're like his pilot group. He appointed those twelve disciples so that they might be with him. One of them, Judas, chose not to be with him in the end and ended up killing himself. The other eleven change the world because they're with God through Jesus.

Then there is what has come to be called the Acts 2 community — the first attempt at church. Jesus has returned to be with his Father, but he is still present through his Holy Spirit. Though he is not present physically, his followers find another way of doing life.

They devote themselves every day to what Jesus taught: to prayer, to fellowship, to breaking of bread together. They shared what they owned; they served each other's needs. Ethnic barriers came down as they became known by the way they loved each other. It's a different community, devoted to a Jesus way of life with God.

NOW IT'S OUR TURN

Over the recent centuries, every once in a while a follower of Jesus gets a vision for this kind of intimate life with God. Centuries ago a man named Nicolas Herman, who was an uneducated household servant from a poor family, got converted to the Christian faith by looking at a tree. It was winter, and the tree was barren, but it occurred to Nicolas that the tree would grow leaves again in the spring. This produced in him a deep sense of God's care and power. It struck him that if God does that for trees, he would surely do it for a person. So this young man entered into a monastic community, spent his life in the kitchen as a cook and dishwasher, and all the while privately devoted his life to being with God.

Today we know him as Brother Lawrence.

When he died, friends gathered some of his letters together and turned them into a book. The book is called *The Practice of the Presence of God*. It was written in the seventeenth century and is now thought to be the most widely read book in the history of the human race other than the Bible — this, from an uneducated dishwasher.

When the soul is with God it doesn't matter if you are a dishwasher or a president. The soul thrives not through our accomplishments but through simply being with God.

Now it's our turn. How do we — ordinary people living in our world of technology and economic challenges, huge moral debates, and rapidly changing beliefs — how do you and I find a Jesus-way to live? How do we discover the "with God" life that we saw in the lives of the disciples, the Acts 2 church, Brother Lawrence, and others before us?

While there are no magic formulas for being with God, lately I have been conducting a little self-test that I call The Soul Experiment. It's a simple way of focusing my soul on God throughout the day. I begin each day by challenging myself: *How many moments of my life today can I fill with conscious awareness of and surrender to God's presence?* Then I try to deliberately imagine myself doing that at home, at work, in my car, when I'm online, when I'm watching the news, when I'm with others. Can I do the "with God" life all the time? I've been trying to make this the goal of my day as opposed to a list of things I have to get done. Can I just keep God in my mind today, regardless of what I'm doing? Here's a little picture of how it works for me.

How many moments of my life today can I fill with conscious awareness of and surrender to God's presence?

One day I had a meeting with my staff that lasted about an hour and a half. When it was over, I realized I had failed for an hour and a half at this experiment. I had not thought about or listened for God a single time in that hour and a half —and I work at a church. Then I had to drive somewhere, and I was grousing in my spirit because I felt like I had too much to do and not enough time to get it done. Do you ever have that kind of thought? I was feeling hurried, impatient, and ill-tempered.

Then this thought came to me: "John, let's look at the next two hours. You will go through those two hours of your life with me or without me. You can continue doing life without me and feel stressed, pressured, angry, sorry for yourself, impatient, and be a pain in the neck to the people around you. You can do those two hours that way. Or you can do those two hours with me. You can be glad you're alive. You can be grateful you were given a life. You can be joyful you actually have work to do, and you can recognize that I, not you, am running the universe. Actually, I was doing pretty well with it before you were ever even born, and I'll probably be able to manage whether or not you think you get your list of things to do done in the next two hours. What's it going to be, John? The next two hours with me or without me?"

When you look at life that way, doesn't it make sense to say,

"Yes, God. I want to do life with you. My soul needs you more than it needs my frustration and impatience."

The "with God" life is not a life of more religious activities or devotions or trying to be good. It is a life of inner peace and contentment for your soul with the maker and manager of the universe. The "without God" life is the opposite. It is death. It will kill your soul.

THE SOUL'S LIFE WITH GOD

Another great pioneer in this experiment in the early twentieth century was a remarkable man named Frank Laubach. This is what he wrote: "For do you not see that God is trying experiments with human lives? That is why there are so many of them.... He has [seven billion] experiments going around the world at this moment. And his question is, 'How far will this man and that woman allow me to carry this hour?' "

How far? I'm not a scientist, but I know that in an experiment, you start by forming a hypothesis. A hypothesis is basically an assumption. It's saying, "I think this is the way it should be." Then you test that assumption by putting it to work, often in a laboratory. Your laboratory is your life — that's where you play out your experiment. When it comes to the soul's life with God, here are three assumptions to put to the test:

God wants to make every moment of my life glorious with his presence. This is the core of the "with God" life. It's not just that he wants to be with us, but that he desires to make our lives "glorious." That's not a word we use often, but it's a great word when we think of the effect being with God can have on our souls. It means basically that he wants to fill our souls with beauty, splendor, wonder, and magnificence. It's what makes people say when they have been with you, "There's something really different about her. She just seems to shine no matter what." But this is not something reserved for the saints of the church or super-spiritual people. God desires this for all of us. That's the whole point of tending to the soul — to fill us so completely with his presence that the brilliance of his love shines through us.

Many Christians expend so much energy and worry trying not to sin. The goal is not to try to sin less. In all your efforts to keep from sinning, what are you focusing on? Sin. God wants you to focus on him. To be with him. "Abide in me." Just relax and learn to enjoy his presence. Every day is a collection of moments, 86,400 seconds in a day. How many of them can you live with God? Start where you are and grow from there. God wants to be with you every moment.

The psalmist says "I have set the LORD always before me." Paul says, "We take captive every thought to make it obedient to Christ." They speak to the need for our souls to be completely and thoroughly with God. But as both of these verses suggest, it does not happen automatically. "Set" and "take captive" are active verbs, implying that you have a role in determining where your soul rests.

I was invited to speak in the chapel of the Naval Academy. It's an old historic, marble, beautiful building. I look out at the front couple of rows, and there is a bunch of young midshipmen all dressed up in their uniforms. They have devoted their lives to trying to serve our country. In that moment I set my thoughts on God, even breathing a silent prayer: "God, I'm so grateful to be here. I'm so grateful there are young people who commit their lives to that." In that moment, I chose to set my thoughts on God.

Before I was introduced, the leader of this service announced the person who was going to be speaking at the next navy chapel. I knew that person and allowed myself to think, "I wish that guy wasn't coming here to speak because he'll give a better talk than me. People will like his talk more than they'll like my talk." This is how quickly we can set our thoughts back on ourselves. But here's the best part of this experiment of seeing how much of each day we can meet the need of our souls to be with God. As soon as I became aware of my self-centeredness, I surrendered my thoughts back to God and enjoyed his presence again. That's just how God works with us—he relentlessly pursues us because all he has ever wanted is to be with us. He reaches out to slaves, people in prison, and people like me doing silly, foolish things and says, "Welcome back."

The best place to start doing life with God is in small moments. I don't know about you, but when I stand on a bluff overlooking the ocean or watch the sunrise over the peaks of a mountain range, it's easy to be "with God." One of my favorite services at our church is Easter Sunday morning, when the place is packed and we sing the great hymns proclaiming the wonder of the resurrection and everyone just beams with adoration for God. No one has to remind me at that moment that God is with me. Unfortunately, those moments are few and far between — every day can't be Easter. Which is why we need to deliberately look for God in the ordinary moments of everyday life.

When I wake up, I invite God to "Be with me this day." Then I try to consciously experience him walking next to me. Not in a magnificent worship experience, but in the ordinary and mundane.

> When I wake up, I invite God to "Be with me this day." Then I try to consciously experience him walking next to me.

My commute can be an ordeal of traffic and delays, or it can be a time to reflect on God. My to-do list for that day can seem overwhelming or deadly boring, or it can remind me that God will be with me in every meeting, every phone call, every deadline. I would like to say I do this well and consistently, but the truth is, sometimes I get in such a rush that I miss noticing and enjoying God's presence in the moment. It often happens in airports.

As I've mentioned before, hurry is one of the major barriers that keeps me from life on the vine. So I have developed all these little tricks to get me through airports as quickly as possible. When I'm getting off a plane, I usually have a computer bag and a suitcase with wheels. The aisles are really narrow, so I hold the computer bag and the suitcase in either hand while I'm going down the aisle. Then when I get into that broader walkway, I put the suitcase down, raise the handle, and put the long strap on the computer bag over the handle so I can wheel the whole thing out easily.

Here is the problem: When I'm doing that, if I pull over to the side of the walkway, people behind pass me — and I feel like they're beating me. Can't let that happen. So as I raise the handle on my suitcase, I sort of swing it around so that it's blocking the walkway, preventing some little old lady or sales rep from passing me. I'm not proud of this.

I was executing this blocking move a few weeks ago when I heard this little whisper: "John, let someone pass you. You're just not that important. I don't need you to hurry, plus it makes you obnoxious to other people. So today, pull over to the side, take a breath, assemble your little luggage cart, and let someone pass you."

I have learned to listen to that still small voice. I did as I was told. I stepped to the side, assembled my bags, and watched three people pass me, and it actually felt good. It felt good to not be in such a hurry. It felt even better to recognize that God was with me. In that small moment. As the rest of the world rushed by.

Sometimes a jetway can become a cathedral.

People will look different when I see them with God. People are a huge part of the "with God" life, because we have to live with people. We have to interact with them. How we get along with people says a lot about where our soul rests. When we are living with God, we will see people as God sees them. If I'm aware God is here with me, and God is looking at you at the same moment I'm looking at you, it will change how I respond to you. Instead of seeing you as the annoying server at McDonald's who messed up my order, I will see you as someone God loved enough to send his Son to die on your behalf. I will see you as a real person who got up dreading going to work, dealing with impatient customers, being on her feet all day. In other words, I will no longer see you as everyone else sees you. This is exactly what Paul is after when he says, "From now on we regard no one from a worldly point of view." From now on, now that my soul is centered with God in Jesus, I won't look at people the same way.

Too often, those of us in the Christian community see people the same way the rest of the world sees them. It's even how we see each other. This is why we feel it necessary to wear masks in church—to present an image that will make them see us the way we want them to see us. It works. One of the most common exchanges between people when they see each other begins with this: "Hi. Good to see you. How are you doing?" And the practiced response is this: "Fine, and you?"

In reality, most of the time things aren't fine, but we would never let anyone know that because we're worried about what they will think of us. How tragic. When you think about it, is there a better place to feel free to be who we are than in church, than with other Christians? If I knew that you would see me the way God sees me, I might feel free to admit, "I'm wrestling with sexual sin, with money, with greed, with anger, with impatience, with my spouse, with my kids, with myself."

Imagine how your church would change if you saw each other through God's eyes. Imagine how the world would respond if Christians saw people the way God sees them.

In the beginning, God created the perfect home for your soul: a garden of perfection where he could be with you. That is all God has ever wanted. Because of our choices, we separated ourselves from God, but he relentlessly pursued us, offering us a way to return to him and be with him. Because we no longer live in that perfect garden, we sometimes forget that he is there, and we continue to live without him.

> *Your soul will never find rest unless it finds its home. We find it in the simple daily discipline of asking ourselves, "Is God here in this moment?" If he is not, he can be.*

Your soul will never find rest unless it finds its home. We find it in the simple daily discipline of asking ourselves, "Is God here in this moment?" If he is not, he can be.

Acknowledge that you have tried once again to live life alone and then welcome him back. Go back to the last scene where you were so joyfully filled with his presence, and then continue the journey.

God invites you to let your soul rest in him.

CHAPTER 11

THE SOUL
NEEDS REST

In the Bible, God never gives anyone an easy job. God never comes
to Abraham, or Moses, or Esther and says, "I'd like you to do me
a favor, but it really shouldn't take much time. I wouldn't want to
inconvenience you." God does not recruit like someone from the
PTA. He is always intrusive, demanding, exhausting. He says we
should expect that the world will be hard, and that our assignments will be hard.

The Bible does use the word *easy* once, though. It came from
Jesus. "Come to me, all you who are weary and burdened ... and
you will find rest for your souls. For my yoke is *easy* and my burden is light." Easy is a soul word, not a circumstance word; not an
assignment word. Aim at having easy circumstances, and life will
be hard all around. Aim at having an easy soul, and your capacity
for tackling hard assignments will actually grow. The soul was not
made for an easy life. The soul was made for an easy yoke.

Years ago, a Christian psychiatrist named Frank Lake worked
with many people who wanted to serve noble causes, but the stress
and demands and difficulties got to them, and soon they became
drained and bitter and cynical and discouraged.

He got together with the great Swiss theologian Emil Brunner,
and they began to reflect on the life of Jesus in the Gospels. Jesus
faced enormous stresses and difficulties and pain. Yet he never got

126

sarcastic or cynical or unloving or burnt out. No one took away his joy.

When they looked at Jesus' life, they saw a pattern to it, different from the pattern of the lives of the missionaries Frank Lake saw burning out. All human beings face challenge and pain and demands. Jesus, however, lived in a divine rhythm where grace was constantly flowing into him and then flowing out from him.

FLOWING IN THE GRACE OF ACCEPTANCE

The beginning movement in the Cycle of Grace is *Acceptance*.

Jesus is brought into the world by a mother who loves him; he is cared for by parents who give him protection and nurture. Before he began his ministry, he was baptized, and when he came up out of the water, a voice spoke from heaven:

You are my Son, whom I love; with you I am well pleased.

For Jesus, identity and acceptance come before achievement and ministry. This is joy no one can take away. You cannot earn acceptance.

Interesting fact: The day on which your sheer existence is celebrated is your birthday. But you get no credit for your role in that event at all. You were never less competent on any day of your life than the day you were born: You were weaker, slower, dumber, slimier, least coordinated, least developed in IQ, and of a higher nuisance factor that day than any other day of your existence.

> *For Jesus, identity and acceptance come before achievement and ministry. This is joy no one can take away. You cannot earn acceptance.*

A birthday is grace. If you have 100 birthdays, you actually get a card from the president of the United States. What did you do? Just didn't die. That's grace.

We forget that the work of our own lives is a gift from our heavenly Father. Jesus never forgot. He heard the voice of heaven.

He heard it again, right before he was to die, on the Mount of Transfiguration: "This is my beloved Son, with whom I am well pleased."

Jesus depended on God's acceptance because he faced massive human rejection. God's acceptance is stronger than human rejection, but it was not just for him. Jesus realized that his acceptance was not just for his own sake.

The alternative to soul-acceptance is soul-fatigue. There is a kind of fatigue that attacks the body. When we stay up too late and rise too early; when we try to fuel ourselves for the day with coffee and a donut in the morning and Red Bull in the afternoon; when we refuse to take the time to exercise and we eat foods that clog our brains and arteries; when we constantly try to guess which line at the grocery store will move faster and which car in which lane at the stoplight will move faster and which parking space is closest to the mall, our bodies grow weary.

There is a kind of fatigue that attacks the mind. When we are bombarded by information all day at work ... When multiple screens are always clamoring for our attention ... When we carry around mental lists of errands not yet done and bills not yet paid and emails not yet replied to ... When we try to push unpleasant emotions under the surface like holding beach balls under the water at a swimming pool ... our minds grow weary.

There is a kind of fatigue that attacks the will. We have so many decisions to make. When we are trying to decide what clothes will create the best possible impression, which foods will bring us the most pleasure, which tasks at work will bring us the most success, which entertainment options will make us the most happy, which people we dare to disappoint, which events we must attend, even what vacation destination will be most enjoyable, the need to make decisions overwhelms us. The sheer length of the menu at Cheesecake Factory oppresses us. Sometimes college students choose double majors, not because they want to study two fields, but simply because they cannot make the decision to say "no" to either one. Our wills grow weary with so many choices.

These categories of fatigue are difficult enough in and of themselves. But they combine to make us feel separated from God, separated from ourselves, and distanced from what we love most about life and creation.

This is soul-fatigue.

RESTING IN SUSTAINING GRACE

The next movement is what might be called *Sustenance*, or sustaining grace. The idea here is that Jesus engaged in certain practices that allowed God's grace to keep replenishing his spirit:

- He prayed.
- He had a circle of close friends — the twelve who went through life with him. He shared everything with them; people underestimate the role of friendship in Jesus' life.
- He engaged in regular corporate worship at synagogue.
- He fed his mind with Scripture.
- He enjoyed God's creation — mountain, garden, and lake.
- He took long walks.
- He welcomed little children and hugged them and blessed them.
- He enjoyed partying with non-religious types.

Notice that the last one — one you might not have thought about — was so much the case that it actually gave rise to rumors about him:

The Son of Man came eating and drinking, and people say, "Here is a glutton and a drunkard, a friend of immoral people."

A common problem is that people think of spiritual practices as obligations that will actually drain them. Sometimes I may need to engage in a practice like giving generously, or serving humbly, which my sinful side resists. But generally I need to engage in practices that connect me to God's grace and energy and joy. That might be going to the ocean, listening to glorious music, being with life-giving friends, taking a long hike—doing them with Jesus.

The test of a sustaining spiritual practice is: Does it fill you with grace for life? What are your sustaining practices? Do you want to explore some new ones?

The soul craves rest. Our wills sometimes rejoice in striving; our bodies were made to (at least sometimes) know the exhilaration of tremendous challenge; our minds get stretched when they must focus even when tired. But the soul craves rest. The soul knows only borrowed strength. The soul was made to rest in God the way a tree rests in soil.

The American devotional writer Lettie Cowman wrote about a traveler visiting Africa and engaging a group of carriers and guides. Hoping to make her journey a swift one, she was pleased with the progress of the many miles they covered that first day. On the second day, though, all the carriers she had hired remained seated and refused to move. She was greatly frustrated and asked the leader of her hired hands why they would not continue the journey. He told her that on the first day they had traveled too far too fast, and now they were waiting for their souls to catch up to their bodies.

> Have you ever felt that you needed the time and space to let your soul catch up with your body? That's a good indication your soul needs rest.

Cowman reflects, "This whirling rushing life which so many of us live does for us what the first march did for those poor jungle tribesmen. The difference: they knew what they needed to restore life's balance; too often we do not."

Have you ever felt that you needed the time and space to let your soul catch up with your body? That's a good indication your soul needs rest.

Psychologist Roy Baumeister has coined the term "ego depletion" to describe a level of fatigue that goes beyond mere physical tiredness. People living in this depleted condition report more tiredness and negative emotions, but those are not the only effects. Depleted people who watch a sad movie become extra sad. When facing temptations like eating chocolate chip cookies, they are more likely to give in. When faced with challenges like an especially difficult assignment at work, they are more likely to fail or turn in lower quality work. The brain area that's crucial for self-control (the anterior cingulate cortex) actually experiences a slowdown.

Soul-fatigue damages our relationships with the people in our lives. Baumeister writes about a therapist who noted that dual-career couples tend to fight over seemingly trivial issues every evening. The therapist advised these couples to go home earlier, which seemed to make little sense — why have more time to fight? But it was the long hours at work that were draining them. They had nothing left to help them overlook their spouse's annoying habits. They were more likely to interpret a spouse's comment in a negative light. They had no energy left for the relationship. They gave it all at the office.

One of the challenges of soul-fatigue is that it does not have the same obvious signs as physical fatigue. If you've run a marathon, your body lets you know it's finished. After mowing the lawn, you're likely to relax with a glass of iced tea because your body tells you it needs rest. My wife hates to put gas in her car. She prides herself on seeing how close to empty she can get before going to a gas station. She has one of those cars with a little screen that will tell you how many miles you can go before you hit empty. Recently she texted me a picture of her dashboard: the screen read that she had 0 miles to go before empty.

The soul was not made to run on empty. But the soul doesn't come with a gauge. The indicators of soul-fatigue are more subtle:

- Things seem to bother you more than they should. Your spouse's gum-chewing suddenly reveals to you a massive character flaw.

- It's hard to make up your mind about even a simple decision.

- Impulses to eat or drink or spend or crave are harder to resist than they otherwise would be.

- You are more likely to favor short-term gains in ways that leave you with high long-term costs. Israel ended up

worshiping a golden calf simply because they grew tired of
having to wait on Moses and God.

- Your judgment is suffering.
- You have less courage. "Fatigue makes cowards of us all"
  is a quote so ubiquitous that it has been attributed to
  General Patton and Vince Lombardi and Shakespeare. The
  same disciples who fled in fear when Jesus was crucified
  eventually sacrificed their lives for him. What changed was
  not their bodies, but their souls.

The soul is not well when we rush so much. If it does not get
the rest it needs, it becomes fatigued. Who better to help me
understand the solution to this problem than my friend Dallas?
For I sincerely believe he was incapable of hurry.

I watched a video recently of an interview I did with Dallas. I
have done this many times; it helps break Dallas's thoughts into
bite-size chunks for those of us who need time to digest. But what
struck me as I watched was how quickly I spoke and how slowly
Dallas responded. You can tell by watching that's he's actually
thinking before he speaks. (Imagine that!) When he finishes one
sentence, there is often a long pause before the next one begins.
I realized while watching that this is one of the reasons it was a
challenge to interview Dallas. You never knew if he was actually
finished talking. He might be done with his response to a question,
or just pausing to reload. I think I could have asked him a single
question, and his answer might never have ended.

It was the same riding in a car with him, or sharing a meal, or
listening to a conversation with a third person. He never rushed a
song, or a walk, or a prayer. Part of the reason people found it healing to be with him was this quality, which was highly contagious.
We think of it as being rested or unhurried, which it is. But it is
the effect resting has on the soul: it gives it peace.

Jesus said, "Peace I leave with you; my peace I give you. I do not
give to you as the world gives. Do not let your hearts be troubled
and do not be afraid." When you give your soul rest, you open it to
the peace Jesus intends for you.

FINDING SIGNIFICANCE OUTSIDE OF PERFORMANCE

The third movement in the Cycle of Grace is *Significance*.

We were made to make a difference beyond ourselves. Significance as it relates to the word *sign*—our lives were meant to be signs that point beyond ourselves to God.

Jesus had great clarity about the significance of his life, often described in his great "I AM" statements: I am the bread of life; I am the Way; I am the Vine; I am the Good Shepherd. The reasons he was here in the world.

Then he would state the significance of his followers, the "You are..." statements: You are the light of the world. You are the salt of the earth. You are a city on a hill.

This third movement involves grace not just flowing into us, but also now through us and out into others for their sake. But this, too, is a gift of God's grace. Do we know who we are, apart from money, power, and reputation?

As Jesus began his ministry, his very first temptation took place after he had been told by the Father, "This is my beloved Son." In the next verse Jesus goes into the wilderness. The Evil One says to him: "IF you are the Son of God, turn these stones into bread.... IF you are the Son of God, throw yourself down from the temple."

In other words: Don't listen to the voice. Don't trust grace. Don't believe your Father. Prove it. Earn it. Make it happen. Make it about you.

Jesus said, "No."

Temptation depended on getting Jesus to question his identity, to feel as if he had to prove his identity by doing spectacular things that would set him apart and mark him out as superior to everybody else.

Significance is about who we are before it is about what we do.

Significance is about who we are before it is about what we do.

My friend Kent is a coach.

My sister Barbie is an encourager and a people-builder; I watched her do this for hours with my daughters not long ago, and I was in awe.

Debbie is a singer and artist who brings healing through beauty. Dave is a connector who makes little families out of strangers.

What is the core part of you God made you to be that they will talk about at your funeral? If you're not clear on this, ask some people who know you well to describe why they think God put you on earth.

The grace of significance liberates me from the need to hurry.

Dallas pointed out to me once that there is a world of difference between being busy and being hurried. Being busy is an outward condition, a condition of the body. It occurs when we have many things to do. Busy-ness is inevitable in modern culture. If you are alive today in North America, you are a busy person. There are limits to how much busy-ness we can tolerate, so we wisely find ways to slow down whenever we can. We take vacations, we sit in a La-Z-Boy® with a good book, we enjoy a leisurely meal with friends. By itself, busy-ness is not lethal.

Being hurried is an inner condition, a condition of the soul. It means to be so preoccupied with myself and my life that I am unable to be fully present with God, with myself, and with other people. I am unable to occupy this present moment. Busy-ness migrates to hurry when we let it squeeze God out of our lives. Note the differences between the two:

Busy	Hurried
A full schedule	Preoccupied
Many activities	Unable to be fully present
An outward condition	An inner condition of the soul
Physically demanding	Spiritually draining
Reminds me I need God	Causes me to be unavailable to God

I cannot live in the kingdom of God with a hurried soul. I cannot rest in God with a hurried soul.

Jesus was often busy, but never hurried. Moreover, he seemed to be quick to detect hurry-sickness in others. Once when he had sent his disciples out on a mission, they returned to him to report what they had done and taught. Imagine being one of Jesus' closest followers given the privilege of sharing his message of love and forgiveness. You just completed a big assignment successfully and are probably a little jazzed about what your next mission will be. It's not like there isn't a lot of work to be done. So many needy people came to Jesus that, according to the Bible, he didn't have a chance to eat. So what assignment does Jesus give his willing followers? "Come with me by yourselves to a quiet place and get some rest." Instead of hurrying off to the next assignment, Jesus got everyone into a boat, and they went off to what was recorded as "a solitary place."

But what about the mission to save the world? What about all the sick people who needed to be healed? I believe Jesus knew the power of a rested soul. He slowed his followers down so that their souls would not become fatigued. We seem to spend most of our time trying to draw crowds and please crowds; Jesus seemed to spend much of his getting away from them.

A rested soul is the easy yoke.

As we learned earlier, our souls exist to integrate our lives so that we can live in harmony with God and the world. They become sick when we are divided and conflicted. I should be content with my job, but I become jealous of someone in the next cubicle because she got the assignment I wanted. I obsess about making more money but to convince myself I am not a greedy person, I tell myself that I am really just trying to provide more security for my family. I become so wrapped up in myself that my choices and values and desires and beliefs are at odds with each other. They are also at odds with other people and with God.

Then I go into nature. I stand on a beach before the ocean. My mind is filled with admiration for the sights and sounds of the waves. Other distracting thoughts melt away. There is congruence between what my body experiences (the sights and sounds of the ocean) and what my mind is thinking (God's beauty and goodness). By slowing down and observing the beauty of my surroundings, I tend not to worry about tomorrow or regret yesterday. I am less enslaved by other people's opinions of me.

There is greater congruence between what I think, feel, choose, and do. I experience, at least for a few moments, what it is to be unconflicted, whole.

My soul gets healed.

Of course, my soul was not made to stand in front of the ocean forever. But I can bring some of that wholeness with me into my divided world. The psalmist says our job is not to heal our souls, but to make space for them so that healing can come. "He makes me lie down in green pastures, he leads me beside quiet waters. He refreshes my soul."

Where are your green pastures? Where are your still waters? I am not an expert on sheep, but I have a friend who raises them. He says that sheep basically do nothing. They eat ... they lie down ... they sleep. They are totally dependent on their shepherd. They do not plan their next meal. They do not make a list of what they have to do tomorrow. Eat. Lie down. Sleep.

Of course, none of us can actually spend all our lives doing nothing. But I think the psalmist uses the metaphor of sheep to make a point. How good are you at doing nothing? How long can you sit in a chair in your backyard and do nothing? Not water the lawn. Not mentally plan the next day. Not worry about your taxes. Just sit and do nothing. By painting this picture of a lamb enjoying whatever his master puts in front of him, we are shown what we need to "refresh our souls." We're generally quite good at doing something, but we're really bad at doing nothing.

The space where we find rest and healing for our souls is solitude.

The world, culture, society—all of this—exerts a relentless, ceaseless, lethal pressure on your soul, and without relief from all of this chaotic interference, the soul dies. J.B. Phillips translates the familiar words of Romans 12:2 to say: "Don't let the world around you squeeze you into its own mould." The world imposes hurry on our souls like a child squeezes a handful of Play-Doh. In solitude we withdraw not so much from creation, but from the pressure of the world. We withdraw so our souls can rest in God. In solitude we remember we are not what anybody thinks of us—we are sheep tended to by the Shepherd.

Solitude provides a shelter from noise and distraction, and that can be scary. We have become almost addicted to both. Have you ever headed out for a nice walk or run an errand and discovered that you left your cell phone behind? If you're like me, you either dashed back to retrieve it or worried the whole time that you were missing an important call.

> *Solitude provides a shelter from noise and distraction, and that can be scary. We have become almost addicted to both.*

Your soul needs rest.

Or you get home early and the house is empty, and you realize you've got about an hour of solitude that your soul desperately needs, so you lie down on the couch and turn on your flat screen to catch the last innings of a baseball game.

Your soul needs rest.

It is not always the "world" that squeezes us into its mold. We all too often distract ourselves. Being completely alone with nothing but our thoughts can be frightening, so we will use anything to distract us from experiencing the soul-healing that comes in solitude. We fear doing nothing because it would mean facing up to the inner realities that distress our souls: fear, anger, loneliness, failure. Perhaps that's why, in the familiar psalm quoted earlier, "He makes me lie down." He doesn't invite us to lie down. He doesn't plead with us to lie down. He makes us. When it comes to the rest we need to restore our souls, we're like our own little children at bedtime. Kids just don't want to go to bed, no matter how tired they are. So at some point as good parents, we pick them up, carry them into their bedrooms, and make them go to bed.

Is it bedtime for your soul?

DOING NOTHING
IS DOING A LOT

The capacity to do nothing is actually evidence of a lot of spiritual growth. The French writer Blaise Pascal wrote centuries ago: "I have discovered that all the unhappiness of men arises from one

single fact, that they are unable to stay quietly in their own room."
In solitude we liberate ourselves from the pressure of the world. You
don't do that by going into solitude with a list of things you want
to work on. You don't even approach solitude with the expectation
that you will come away with some deep spiritual insight. It's not
about what you're going to do; it's about what you're *not* going to
do. In solitude you rest.

Back in the garden, the perfect home for the soul, God modeled
for us the need for rest: "God had finished the work he had been
doing; so on the seventh day he rested from all his work." Later in
his journey with mankind, he made rest one of the ten uncompro-
mising directives for how we should live: "Remember the Sabbath
day by keeping it holy.... On it you shall not do any work." Spend
one day a week, one seventh of your time, doing nothing. I love
how the late evangelist Vance Havner wrote about the soul's need
for rest: "If you don't come apart for a while, you will come apart
in a while."

Abraham Heschel wrote: "Six days a week we wrestle with the
world, wringing profit from the earth; on the Sabbath we especially care for the seed of eternity planted in the soul. The world
has our hands, but our soul belongs to Someone Else. Six days a
week we seek to dominate the world, on the seventh day we try to
dominate the self...."

Christians of my generation, and especially those preceding
mine, recall Sundays (the Sabbath to most Protestants) as being
pretty boring. About all that was allowed was going to church,
reading the Bible, and taking naps. No playing sports on Sunday.
No TV on Sunday. No commerce on Sunday—if you ran out of
gas on the way to church or needed to buy a gallon of milk, tough
luck. I am grateful that in our wisdom we have abandoned such
legalism, but the notion of rest was—and still is—God's idea.

RESTING IN ACHIEVEMENT

The final phase of the Cycle of Grace is *Achievement.* Jesus achieved a great deal. He taught, healed, befriended, recruited, trained, traveled, confronted, defied, and launched the greatest movement in human history. To achieve — to bear fruit — is crucial to the soul. But fruitfulness is just as much a matter of grace as acceptance is. The fruitful soul is also a Sabbath-soul.

There is another way of looking at the Sabbath that may seem to contradict what I just wrote, but it bears examining. I have always wondered, if God is omnipotent, why would he need to rest? The most common answer I've heard is the one I just outlined: that he did it as an example for people to follow. But there are many commands he gives to the human race that he doesn't follow — starting with the first one about being fruitful and multiplying.

There is another answer that also has something to say about soul rest. Old Testament scholar John Walton notes that the entire creation story in Genesis is set against the backdrop of sacred space. Just as a seven-day framework is set up in Genesis, royal temples or sacred palaces were inaugurated during seven-day festivals. In Eden, God himself created a garden. Kings often had gardens outside their residences. God uses the same kind of language that kings used in their kingdoms. A king says, "Let there be taxes," and there are taxes.

When a temple or a palace was inaugurated, it symbolized the victory of the king. When his enemies were subdued, he could leave the battle, enter the temple, and rest on his throne.

A throne is where a king rested.

It didn't mean he was taking the day off. It meant that there was no crisis or battle in his kingdom, that he would be able to rule with wisdom and justice and delight. Everyone wanted the king to be able to rest on his throne.

That's why God rested. It didn't mean he took the day off. Everything was the way he intended it to be in his sacred space — what we know as the universe. He could reign with ease and delight.

FREEDOM FROM
THE CYCLE OF WORKS

The opposite of the Cycle of Grace is what might be called the Cycle of Works. In this, I simply go backward against the tide of grace. I begin by trying to achieve impressive accomplishments through my own strength for my own ego. I hope that by doing this I might feel significant.

I hope that this sense of significance will sustain me through all the difficulties and stresses of life. And ultimately I hope that the end result will be a life that is somehow acceptable to somebody.

The Cycle of Works will destroy my soul. It is the hard yoke. It is the heavy burden.

But when your soul is at rest, it occupies the throne of your life. Your will is undivided and obeys God with joy. Your mind has thoughts of truth and beauty. You desire what is wholesome and good. Your body is filled with appetites that serve the good and with habits that lead you into excellent living.

When your soul is at rest, your will is undivided and obeys God with joy. Your mind has thoughts of truth and beauty. You desire what is wholesome and good.

Your soul is at rest.

Whether with an entire day, or periods of time set aside every day, your soul needs rest. Not a change of scenery or a spiritual retreat — those are fine and may *contribute* to rest. But to remain healthy, our souls need solitude with no agenda, no distractions, no noise. If someone asks you what you did in your "time apart," the correct response should be, "Nothing."

Doing nothing does wonders for the soul.

CHAPTER 12

THE SOUL NEEDS FREEDOM

The law of the LORD is perfect, refreshing the soul.
PSALM 19:7

Really?

"They delight in doing everything God wants them to, and day and night are always meditating on his laws and thinking about ways to follow him more closely."

Don't they have anything else to do?

The old masters of the life of the soul used to warn about the dangers of dis-ordered attachment. Desire is good, but when you want something too much, it threatens to take God's place in your life. It will lead you to make bad decisions. It will put you on an emotional roller coaster. The ability to have anything you want actually can cost you your freedom.

> Desire is good, but when you want something too much, it threatens to take God's place in your life. It will lead you to make bad decisions. and put you on an emotional roller coaster.

Samson had an unquenchable desire for Delilah; the rich young ruler was consumed by his desire for money; Saul coveted the power that came with his throne; Cain gave in to his desire for revenge. How did that work for them?

In the movie *A Christmas Story*, one of the kids is given a double-dog dare to touch his tongue to a frozen flagpole on a December morning. Instantly, his tongue is frozen fast to the icy metal, and from that moment he isn't going anywhere. He is stuck. A slave to his tongue. Freedom will come, if it comes at all, only with enormous pain.

We get double-dog dared all the time. Make it about sex. Make it about money. Make it about security. That tender object stuck frozen to the flagpole is your soul. It craves to be free, but we're not sure what that means.

CONFLICTED ABOUT FREEDOM

Imagine you were driving, and a squad car pulled you over for going too fast, and you explained to the officer, "I just don't feel authentic going only sixty-five miles an hour. When I drive, I try to be guided by my deep inner voice, and my deep inner voice was telling me today, 'You can go ninety. You *should* go ninety.' So, officer, don't try to impose your rules on me. When I'm driving, I have to be free!" We have a word to describe these people: speeders. Or crazy.

Imagine an IRS agent knocks on your door. He says, "The government has noticed you haven't paid any taxes for the last ten years." Indignant, you respond, "I understand that paying taxes may work for other people, but not for me. It would feel kind of hypocritical. If I were going to give some of my money to the government, it would not reflect my deepest passions and values. So don't impose your rules on my money. I have to be free!" We have two words to describe these people: tax evaders.

Finally, imagine a man dating a woman, and as they enjoy a nice romantic meal, he leans closer and says, "Being faithful to just one woman would be too confining. I have grown to be in touch with my core inner self, and when my core inner self sees a woman around who's really, really attractive, it wants to stare and chase and see if it can get her to respond." We have a name for these people. We call them ... I'm not even going to go there. You can vote on this one yourself.

The soul cries out to be free, but the common perception is that Christianity stands in the way of freedom. It's all about obeying someone or something that tries to tell you how to live your life. As a Christian, according to this perception, you're not free at all, but submissive, dependent, and enslaved by your religion. So people wonder — does God infringe on your soul's need for freedom? Does becoming a Christian mean somebody dictates what you do, what you think, how you live? Even Christians sometimes adopt this view. They may affirm their belief in Jesus as the Son of God and accept his gift of salvation, but retain their "freedom" to decide for themselves how they should live.

The soul needs freedom, but what exactly does that mean? That I can do whatever I want?

People believe Christianity is too restrictive, because too often, that's the way Christians have lived. We do not delight in the law of the Lord; we delight in keeping it better than other people, or using it to prop up our sense of being "set apart," more pure than the rest of the world. Part of what inspired Philip Yancey's wonderful book *What's So Amazing about Grace?* is the pain he experienced over his church's legalism: "I came out of a Southern fundamentalist culture that frowned on co-ed swimming, wearing shorts, jewelry or makeup, dancing, bowling, and reading the Sunday newspaper. Alcohol was a sin of a different order, with the sulfurous stench of hellfire about it.... No short skirts for women, no longer hair for men, no polka dots on dresses for women because they might draw attention to suggestive body parts, no kissing, no holding hands, no rock music, no facial hair ... it all calls to mind the dog who thought his name was 'No' because that's the only word he ever heard from his master."

Sometimes the church has tried to inflict its rules on broader society. Historian William Manchester records some of the "no's" of John Calvin's Geneva: no "feasting, dancing, singing, pictures, statues, relics, church bells, organs, altar candles, 'indecent or irreligious songs,' staging or attending theatrical plays, wearing rouge, jewelry, lace or 'immodest' dress ... naming children after anyone but figures in the Old Testament."

The law revives the soul? Seems more like the law oppresses the soul. True, rules may be required for a society to survive, although we generally want them to be the minimum required to protect innocent people from harm. Why would anybody think a soul might delight in them? Could it be there is a connection between the law and the soul that is not apparent to us?

The soul craves to be free, but soul-freedom turns out to be a little more complicated than we think.

OBEDIENCE PRODUCES FREEDOM

Israel has always revered the giving of the law in a way that is hard for most of the rest of us — even Christians — to understand. Before giving Moses the Ten Commandments to deliver to Israel, God offered this significant reminder: "I am the LORD your God, who brought you out of Egypt, out of the land of slavery." He could have said, "Here is a list of rules and you better obey them or else." Or he could have said, "I am the Lord your God and I expect you to do exactly what I tell you to do." Instead, he introduced "the Law" by reminding them: "I am your liberator."

The Ten Commandments were never designed to be a stand-alone list of rules. They come within a relational context. They describe what living up to a certain value and a certain identity and a certain destiny looks like. In fact, in Judaism, they are not called the Ten Commandments. The Hebrew term is *aseret hadevarim*, which literally means "ten utterances" or "ten statements" because they were rooted in things that are meant to be in God's kingdom. They flow out of how we were designed, who we were meant to be. We read them as "this is what you have to do," but God was saying, "this is who you are." That's why we don't so much break the Ten Commandments as we break ourselves when we violate them.

> The Ten Commandments flow out of how we were designed, who we were meant to be. That's why we don't so much break them as we break ourselves when we violate them.

Revelation elsewhere in the Bible comes to individuals. God comes to Noah. God comes to Abraham. These ten statements are the only place in all recorded history where he comes to an entire people. This became so formative to Israel that in later centuries, Jewish people would trace their ancestry back to their ancestors at Sinai, the way that people in America trace their roots to the *Mayflower*.

As Moses met with God on Mount Sinai, we are told, the people of Israel "stood at the foot of the mountain." To this day in Judaism, people will stand for the reading of the Ten Commandments. There's a wonderful saying in the *Talmud*: "Every Jewish soul was present at Sinai."

When these words — these commandments — were given to Israel, had they just traded in one form of slavery for another? They used to be bound to Pharaoh; now they're bound to Yahweh. Were they still not free? When we bind ourselves to God, to a code of morality that transcends our own particular opinions, do we lose freedom, or do we gain freedom? If my soul needs freedom, what does the law have to do with it? I believe the soul is actually revived by law.

OBEDIENCE TO GOD
INCREASES FREEDOM

Think of freedom coming in two flavors, two kinds of freedom. There is freedom from external constraints, somebody telling me what to do. This is freedom *from*. But there is another kind of freedom that might be called freedom *for*. There's the freedom for living the kind of life I was made to live, freedom for becoming that man I most want to be — freedom *for*.

You do not have to be an expert to recognize that the kind of freedom our culture craves is freedom from external restraints. Tell someone he can't do something, and he'll probably find a way to do it. Sometimes just for the fun of it, if Nancy and I are in bed and about to go to sleep and she reaches to turn out the lamp, I'll say to her, "I command you to turn off that light. You must obey me."

Sometimes she'll leave that light on all night long just to make the point that I'm not her boss.

You're not the boss of me! Freedom from external restraints appeals to all of us, but I do not believe that it's the freedom the soul needs. For example, you generally can drink as much alcohol as you want, restricted only by laws prohibiting drinking and driving and public drunkenness. But if you want to get loaded every night in the privacy of your home, you're free to have at it. Eventually, however, your drinking will begin to cause problems for you. It damages your health. It embarrasses your kids. It hurts your marriage. It threatens your job. You get to a point where you want to quit but you can't. You discover that you are *not* free to enjoy sobriety. You're free to drink as much as you want, but you're not free to not drink.

"I brought you out of Egypt, out of the land of slavery."

Your freedom is not restricted simply by external constraints. There's another odd kind of restriction. Your freedom gets limited by an internal reality that is a kind of brokenness or weakness or dividedness inside you. You want to stop drinking, but you can't. You want to live with a happy, cheerful, optimistic attitude, but you don't. You want to quit yelling at your kids, but you fail. You want to be the kind of person who manages anger really, really well, but you aren't. You'd like to think you have become unselfish, but you haven't. You are not free. The freedom you lack is an internal freedom, and this inner lack of freedom is much more dehumanizing, much more tragic than external constraints.

This kind of freedom is internal, and it is precious. It is "soul-freedom." Remember that the soul is what integrates our parts. If our will is enslaved to our appetites, if our thoughts are obsessed with unfulfilled desires, if our emotions are slaves to our circumstances, if our bodily habits contradict our professed values, the soul is not free. The only way for the soul to be free is for all the parts of our personhood to be rightly ordered.

When Nelson Mandela was imprisoned by captors, he did not have very much freedom *from*, but there was a freedom inside him that was much greater than what his guards had. The deeper freedom—the freedom that the soul needs—is the freedom *for* becoming the person I was designed to be.

The soul sits in its own prison, having locked the door and, to its surprise, thrown away the key.

FINDING FREEDOM FOR YOUR SOUL

How do you get the freedom that your soul craves? This is the great irony about freedom. To become truly free, you must surrender. Surrender is not a popular concept. It goes against everything we think we know about being free. Wars are not won by surrendering—have you ever seen a football team surrender in the Super Bowl? But surrender is the only way to achieve freedom for your soul.

The alcoholic admits she lacks the willpower to quit drinking. She surrenders her will—her freedom—to a higher power, and through that act of surrender receives power to be free not to drink. It is a model that has healed millions of people through Alcoholics Anonymous, and it is not limited to the abuse of alcohol. If you want to free your soul, you acknowledge that there is a spiritual order that God has designed *for* you. You are not the center of the universe. You are not the master of your fate. You are not the captain of your ship. There is a God, and you aren't him. True freedom comes when you embrace God's overall design for the world and your place in it. This is why in the Bible you see this strong connection between God's law and soul-freedom.

The psalmist writes, "I will always obey your law, for ever and ever." Then the very next verse says, "I will walk about in freedom, for I have sought out your precepts." Or, in the book of James we find that "whoever looks intently into the perfect law that gives freedom, and continues in it—not forgetting what they have heard, but doing it—they will

> *True freedom comes when you embrace God's overall design for the world and your place in it. This is why in the Bible you see this strong connection between God's law and soul-freedom.*

be blessed in what they do." God's law was given to us not to force us to obey a list of rules, but to free our souls to live full and blessed.

The enslaved soul is sick and needs reviving. In the early centuries of the church, people began to speak of the "cure of the soul." One of the early church fathers wrote, "For the cure [sometimes translated as "care"] of the soul, the most variable and manifold of creatures, seems to me in very deed to be the art of arts and science of sciences." He goes on to say that the cure of souls is harder work, more important than healing bodies. Sometimes when we use a therapeutic word like *healing*, it can sound as if we're only talking about the wounds and the scars and the hurts we carry around. We do all have those. It's good to be open about them, but at the core, the disease that really threatens our soul is sin. I am complicit in the sickness of my soul in a different way than in diseases that attack my body. I say yes to greed and lust in a way I don't say yes to colds and strep throat.

The sickness that denies the soul its freedom responds poorly to conventional treatment. The late American sociologist Philip Rieff suggests that we have adopted a secularized, therapeutic framework for viewing life that ignores the needs of the soul. "Religious man was born to be saved; psychological man is born to be pleased."

SIN, FREEDOM, AND THE SOUL

To understand how the soul becomes enslaved and where freedom truly lies, we need to consider three different levels where the soul gets trapped. One way to think of this is to imagine a target with three concentric circles moving from the outer edge to the bull's eye.

Sinful acts. These are particular behaviors: We lie. We cheat on a test. We gossip about somebody. We yell at somebody when "it's not fair." We are able to commit these sins every day without remorse, thanks to a tool without which we could not survive given the reality of our souls: denial. A friend of mine commissioned the Barna research group to do a national survey on the top temptations people say they face when it comes to sin. This was done anonymously online, so respondents didn't have to worry about anyone discovering their deep, dark sins. Hatred, abuse, racism, breakdown of families, rampant greed, dishonesty, violence. According to their honest answers, what do you think are the most destructive temptations facing the human soul today? Lust? Greed? Hatred? Jealousy? Dishonesty? Pornography?

Here's what we *say* they are:

Number one: worry. "I'm tempted to worry too much. I guess I'll have to confess I just don't trust God as courageously as I should." Number two: procrastination. "Sometimes I put things off." Number three: overeating. "Sometimes I eat too much." Number four: Facebook and Twitter. "I guess I'd have to confess sometimes I use social media too much if I want to be really brutally honest about myself." Number five: laziness. "I can waste a lot of time doing nothing."

Even with a guarantee of never being found out, we can't bear to tell the truth about our sins. Sadly, the soul enslaved by sinful acts cannot be healed if we deny that those acts are really our responsibility.

The King James translation of James 1:21 doesn't mince words: "Wherefore lay apart all filthiness and superfluity of naughtiness." We don't recognize ourselves in those words. Filthiness? What's that? Naughtiness, related to that old word *naught*, means we have amounted to nothing? Those are sinful acts, but if we don't recognize them in ourselves they will continue to enslave our souls.

Sinfulness. The next ring on our target goes deeper and has to do with our orientation. The Bible will in some places address sins, but in other places will address *sin*. Sin is a deeply entrenched pattern way below the surface, insidious — like a disease that just leaks out of us without any effort. My sinful acts are premeditated; my sinfulness is more like a habit I can't control. Self-serving words that just come out of my mouth, even when I'm not trying to promote myself. The way I'll cater to somebody because I think they're important or attractive or wealthy when I don't even like that quality in me. I don't know how to turn it off. I don't know how to shut it down. It's in my body. Jealous attitudes. Chronic ingratitude that just crops up. These thoughts that come into my mind.

Paul says, "I do not understand what I do. For what I want to do I do not do, but what I hate I do.... For I do not do the good I want to do, but the evil I do not want to do—this I keep on doing." Now these are incredibly important words, especially "this I keep on doing." Sinfulness is the habit of sinning.

A habit is a relatively permanent pattern of behavior that allows you to navigate the world. The capacity for habitual behavior is indispensable for human life. When you learn how to type or tie a shoe or play the piano or drive a car, it's hard work. You have to concentrate on it. After you learn, it becomes habitual. It's in your body. Good habits are enormously freeing—we accomplish good things almost on autopilot. One study from Duke University found that more than 40 percent of the actions people take every day aren't decisions, but habits.

Good habits free us, but when sin becomes a habit, our souls lose their freedom.

When Paul says there is nothing good in your sinful nature, he is not talking about a ghost inside you someplace that's fighting it out with another ghost somewhere. He's a brilliant student of human life who knows that sin, evil, wickedness, deception, pride, greed, racism, anger, and ingratitude have become second nature to us all.

You can override a habit by willpower for a moment or two. You go to church. Read the Bible. Worship. Sing. Pray. You feel at peace with God for a moment, and then your sin habit returns. Habits eat willpower for breakfast.

Our only hope is not for more willpower; it is for a new set of habits. Richard Foster told me once that the theologian Thomas Aquinas devoted over seventy pages of his writings to the cultivation of holy habits. Also, the Alcoholics Anonymous 12 Steps are all about acquiring new habits through which we have access to God's power to do what willpower can never do.

Our only hope is not for more willpower; it is for a new set of habits.

This is what the cure of souls looked like for Jesus' followers. They confessed their sins to each other, prayed, and studied the Scriptures together. They replaced sinful habits with new habits — Jesus habits. They met and broke bread together, not as an obligation, but for survival. Soul survival.

Original sin. This is the bull's eye — the explanation for why we sin in the first place. We can't help ourselves. The phrase "original sin" is not actually in the Bible, but the story of humanity's fall from God's grace in the garden describes our condition. Something is broken or wrong with our very nature. There is a leaning toward sin in human beings that's just there.

Mere human efforts (education, environment, therapy) cannot cure the sin problem. My brokenness, like yours, is very complex. Parts of it have to do with my wounds and my scars and my disappointments, but at the core is my natural inclination toward sin. It is deeply embedded in our souls, and it is literally killing us. We cannot change this condition, but we can free our souls from its power over us by recognizing that it is there, daily seeking God's forgiveness and strength, and living the way he designed us.

It is only when we surrender to God and his ways that our souls experience freedom. We may stumble along the way, for no one is perfect. But we serve a perfect Savior who is patient and always ready to forgive us when we fail.

When evangelist Billy Graham's wife, Ruth, died in 2007, she chose to have engraved on her gravestone words that had nothing to do with her remarkable achievements. It had to do with the fact that as long as we are alive, God will be working on us, and then we will be free. She had been driving one day along a highway through a construction site, and there were miles of detours and cautionary signs and machinery and equipment. She finally came to the last one, and this final sign read, "End of construction. Thank you for your patience." That's what is written over Ruth Graham's grave: "End of construction. Thank you for your patience."

Construction today. Freedom tomorrow.

CHAPTER 13

THE SOUL
NEEDS BLESSING

A great surgeon named Richard Selzer had to cut into the face of a lovely young woman to remove a large tumor. He did the best he could, but in the course of the surgery, he severed a tiny twig of a facial nerve that controlled one of the muscles of her mouth. Her once lovely face would remain grotesquely twisted in disfigurement for the rest of her life. Before the surgery, she had that kind of face that would sometimes cause people to just stop and look at it because it was so lovely. No one would ever do that again. If they stopped to look at her face from that day on, it would be for another reason.

Her young husband was beside her hospital bed when she asked for a mirror. As she looked into it, she asked Selzer, "Will my face always look like this?" "Yes," he replied. "It will, because the nerve was cut."

She was silent, but her husband smiled. "I like it," he said. "It is kind of cute." And then, to add an exclamation point, he bent down to kiss her crooked mouth. Selzer wrote, "I am so close I can see how he twists his own lips to accommodate to hers to show her their kiss still works."

To show her their kiss still works.

Selzer concluded, "I know it is the marred and the scarred and the faulty that are subject to grace. I would seek the soul.... Yes, it is the exact location of the soul I am after. I have caught glimpses of it...."

The soul is seen when it reaches out in love. The Bible's word for this is blessing.

My friend Dallas used to tell me, "Churches should do seminars on how to bless and not curse others." I thought that was simply a cute saying. I should have known better, but for me, blessing had become an irremediably trite church cliché. Somebody sneezes and someone else will thoughtlessly say, "God bless you," although we'd be surprised if God actually did. Or it becomes a way to dress gossip up in Sunday clothes: "She can't take care of her own children, God bless her." It's a phrase pastors used at the door on Sunday after the service when they felt they should say something spiritual but they didn't know what else to say. Or it's a safe hospital prayer: If I pray "God heal this cancer," my reputation is on the line, but if I pray for blessing, it's hard for anyone to prove I'm a prayer-failure.

Then one day I got a seminar from Dallas on how to bless. I was with my wife and daughter. There were other people in the room, but this was really for us. There are two great words in the Bible, Dallas said, that describe the posture of our souls toward other people. One is to bless. The other is to curse. We are creatures with wills, and in every encounter with other people we will what is good for them, or we fail to do so: we will what is bad. We cannot help ourselves.

> We are creatures with wills, and in every encounter with other people we will what is good for them, or we fail to do so: we will what is bad.

Blessing is not just a word. Blessing is the projection of good into the life of another. We must think it, and feel it, and will it. We communicate it with our bodies. Blessing is kind of like an ancient dance of the Hokey-Pokey; before you finish you have to "put your whole self in."

Blessing is done by the soul.

In Genesis, Isaac was about to give his blessing to his son. He asked his son to prepare him a meal first and give it to him to eat, "that my soul may bless you before I die." The idea that the blessing comes from the soul is repeated again later in the story when Jacob sneaks in to appropriate the blessing that would have gone to his brother Esau. "I will eat of my son's venison that my soul may bless you."

It's instructive that Isaac wants food so that he can bless—will the good. Psychologist Roy Baumeister—the preeminent researcher on willpower in our day—notes that the single greatest predictor of whether judges will "bless" convicts with parole is how recently they (the judges) have eaten. The word *soul* returns when Esau found out what had happened, and asked that his father's soul may bless *him*. This sequence of eating/soul-blessing is repeated three times (Gen. 27:19, 25, 31). By eating, Isaac "increases" his soul. In the blessing the soul "forcefully expresses itself to empower the soul of the other."

In each case, it is not simply Isaac who blesses. The blessing comes from Isaac's soul. It is so deep and real that once it has been given, it cannot be revoked. It is so deeply desired that Esau is panic-stricken at the prospect of losing it: "Bless me, even me also, O my father."

LEARNING TO BLESS

So we sat together, my wife and my oldest daughter, Laura, and I, as Dallas taught us how to bless. He began by quoting the world's oldest blessing, which God gave to Aaron to bless the people of Israel. "You can change the wording if you want," Dallas said, "but it's hard to improve on God."

> The LORD bless you and keep you;
> The LORD make his face to shine upon you, and be gracious
>   to you;
> The LORD lift up his countenance upon you and give you
>   peace.

Blessing and cursing are not compartmentalized Bible words

at all. They are simply the two ways we treat people. They are as inescapable as breathing out and breathing in.

We are acutely sensitive in our souls to being blessed or being cursed. I was driving in downtown Menlo Park, coming out of a meeting where we were making ministry plans to help people learn the love of God. I was getting ready to make a left-hand turn. A driver coming from my right didn't have her turn signal on, so I thought she would go past. I began to inch forward to make my turn. It turns out she *did* turn left, but because I had inched forward she had to adjust her turn. She just glared at me with that expression that says, "Don't you know how to drive?"

I found myself getting angry immediately. She was condemning me, and the human heart hates to be condemned. I wanted to jump out of my car, force her to stop, and scream: "It wasn't *my* fault; it was *your* fault—*you* didn't use your turn signal; but now you're blaming *me*! How dare you?" I even wanted to add, "Your heart is wicked and deceitful above all things!"

I didn't say anything because it just wasn't practical to do that on the street, and because I recognized her—she goes to my church. So I just gave her the blessing sign.

I used to think cursing someone meant swearing at them, or putting a hex on them, so it was pretty easy to avoid because I do not swear much or do hexes. But as I listened to Dallas, I realized how wrong I had been. You can curse someone with an eyebrow. You can curse someone with a shrugged shoulder. I have seen a husband curse a wife by leaving just the tiniest delay before saying, "Of course I love you." The better you know someone, the more subtly and cruelly you can curse them.

The reason we are so sensitive, Dallas said, is that our souls were made to be blessed and cannot survive without the blessing. So he continued to instruct us in how to do it.

Blessing takes time, so don't hurry. One of the difficulties of blessing nowadays is that you may have to grab on to someone to get them to hold still long enough to receive it. Receiving a blessing is as much an art as giving one. We think we're unworthy, or we start to plan on giving a blessing back. Blessing-giving should be asymmetrical. It's not a form of barter. It's grace.

Turn to the one you want to bless. Look into their eyes. You are not simply blessing anyone at random. Allow your mind to focus on this particular individual, the one before you.

Receiving a blessing is as much art as giving one. Blessing-giving should be asymmetrical. It's not a form of barter. It's grace.

"The Lord bless you …" This means, may the Lord constantly bring good into your life. Like food goes into the body, words go into the soul. When Laura was a child, some of our words were words of blessing. When she cried in her crib in the middle of the night, I would walk into her room and say, "I'll stroke your little head." I would bend over her and massage her soft hair until my back ached, and begin to tiptoe away in the hope that she was asleep. She was never asleep. "Stroke your little head?" she would lisp, and I would bend down once more. I was blessing her, though I did not know to call it that.

But I thought, as I looked into the eyes of my redheaded married daughter, of how I had so often placed on her the pressures of a firstborn to perform in a way that would make me feel successful as a dad. I cringe sometimes when I watch family movies when she was a year old: "Say your words, honey … Say what noises animals make … Perform …" When Laura was going into second grade, I heard her tell a group of people how anxious she was at the start of a school year, how she would feel panicky in her stomach. How cute that she is talking like adults talk, I thought. I had no idea how much anxiety that little soul felt; how acutely it would come to haunt her in later years. She bore it alone, because I did not know, because in many ways I added to it.

Those memories—and a million more—of joy and sorrow, of pride and regret, filled my mind and my heart as I looked into her eyes. "The Lord bless you …"

"The Lord … keep you." Dallas says this means I am willing that God should protect her; that the care and sacrificial love of

Christ poured out on the cross should guard all that is sacred and precious about her. Think about these words that you say, Dallas told us. Look in their eyes. Underline the word *you*.

"The Lord make his face to shine upon you." If you wonder about this, Dallas said, think about the face of a grandparent doting on a grandchild. Dallas has one granddaughter, and she was with us at the time. I looked at her face as he said these words. She was beaming, shining.

"Your face was meant to shine," he said. "Glory always shines. Glory was meant to be shared."

"The Lord lift his countenance upon you ..." Lifting up a countenance is what we do to let someone know we are fully present. It is an act of self-giving. The first time I tried to kiss Nancy, she turned her face to the side so all I got was a section of her cheek to kiss. But the day came when she did not turn to the side, when she "lifted up her countenance" to me.

"And give you peace." Unthreatened, undisturbed peace. As I looked into my daughter's eyes and said this — the same eyes I remember looking into proudly for the first time more than two-and-a-half decades ago — they filled with tears. And so did mine.

And the soul felt its worth.

A SOUL IS WORTH BLESSING

In the book of Exodus, God says to his people, "You shall not oppress a stranger; you know the soul of a stranger, for you were strangers in the land of Egypt." Those are amazing words. Everybody has a soul. We demean people when we forget they have the depth and dignity of a soul. Even the people I don't like have souls. The soul cries out for connection. To love someone with your soul means your will, your choices, your mind, your thoughts, your feelings, your body, your behaviors, and your habits are aligned for the good of their entire being before God. We bless the soul when we love that way. That's soul love.

There is the soul love of friends, perhaps most remarkably recorded in the biblical story of Jonathan and David. "The soul of Jonathan became attached to the soul of David. Jonathan loved him as his own soul. Jonathan made a covenant with David because he loved him as he loved his own soul. Jonathan took off the cloak he was wearing and gave it to David, and his armor too; indeed even his sword, his bow plus his belt." This covenant—an act of the will—is so deep that Jonathan gave David his armor; a symbolic way of telling David that he (David) will become king one day, and that Jonathan assents to this from the depths of his being. Jonathan will seek the good of David at the cost of his ambition and the risk of his life. He will disadvantage himself for the good of his friend.

The soul of one person can become intertwined with the soul of another. Aristotle is supposed to have said: "What is friendship? It is a single soul dwelling in two bodies." The ancient term for such a relationship is "soul friend," defined as one with whom I have no secrets. The ancient Celtic Christians said that "a person without a soul friend is like a body without a head."

The depth of romantic, sexual love demands soul language. The bride in the Song of Solomon calls the other "[he] whom my soul loves." Sex is deeply soulful. Sex focuses body, mind, and will in a unique way. The soul connects and integrates, and sexual union is like none other. The reason we are called to reserve sexual intimacy for marriage is that it honors the soul.

We also see soul love in the love of a parent for a child. I have a friend in Chicago named Joel, who grew up on a little farm. He contracted polio when he was ten months old, so for Joel, walking has always been really, really laborious. He has never run a single step in his whole life, and he is now in his fifties. Joel has a son named Evan. Guess what sport Evan grew up to love? Track. He loves to run competitively and became quite good, and Joel would occasionally email me photos of his son competing, including some of Evan competing in the steeplechase at the U.S. Olympic Trials. There was Evan in a green jersey, ahead of the pack as he crossed the finish line with a look of determination and joy and something else on his face that lights up everyone who watches. He represented the United States in the 2012 Summer Olympics, and if you saw him run and looked real close, you saw my friend's soul running along with him.

The soul is that way. Joel, who could never run, is sitting up in the stands. His soul is down on the track there, running with his boy.

You see manifestations of that with parents and their kids every-

> The soul is that way. Joel, who could never run, is sitting up in the stands. His soul is down on the track there, running with his boy.

where. Have you ever watched a mom or dad at a school concert where their child is singing? What are the parents doing? Mouthing the same words their child is singing. The soul goes out in love.

WIRED TO BLESS

Researchers have actually found what are sometimes called "mirror neurons" that indicate we are wired to bless. When we watch another person perform an action, we have neurons that fire just as if we ourselves were performing that action. Researchers speculate that this allows us to learn by imitation, but also to have empathy for other people. Actually, brain studies are teaching us even more about the soul than that. When we watch another person suffer, a part deep in the brain behind the temples called the anterior cingulate cortex (ACC) burns with activity. The greater the distress, the brighter the ACC burns. However, activity in the ACC does not predict altruism. That is predicted by activity in another part of the brain (dmFPC—don't ask). It turns out that we are most likely to actually help someone, not simply when we see them suffer, but when we also consider ourselves "attached" to them (this is what the dmFPC activity indicates).

Seeing suffering does not move me to act if I think of the person as "him." (Remember the priest and the Levite in the parable of the good Samaritan.) But when I think of that person as part of "us," part of "me," then I am moved to bless. Jesus may have been speaking quite literally when he said, "Love your neighbor as yourself."

What if our souls went out in humble love to all the people God brings into our world? Undeserving, but loved. The soul blesses by loving. Our souls need blessing.

CHAPTER 14

THE SOUL NEEDS SATISFACTION

Best-selling author Michael Singer writes that, in case you haven't noticed it, there is a little mental dialogue going on inside your head all the time. Here's a sample: "Why did she look at me like that? I'll bet she doesn't like me—I've never liked her. I don't know why she got to have him for a husband though; I'd be happy with a husband like that...." On and on it goes. That little voice inside our heads never stops.

Right now, you may be hearing, "What voice? There's no voice going on inside my head." That's the voice I'm talking about. And if you're wondering what it wants, the answer is easy. It wants more. Always more.

The beloved, eighty-something founding elder of the church where I worked was for decades a New Testament professor named Dr. Gilbert Bilezikian. We all called him "Dr. B." He used to walk from his house to Wheaton College, where he worked. I actually had him for a class when I was a student there. One day while he was on his way to the college, he noticed a neighbor had put a sign out in front of his door. It was a beautiful, very artistic, creative sign bearing the street name and address on it. Dr. B., born in France, had always loved beauty. (He said to my wife one day, in his dapper Inspector Clouseau voice, "You are looking particularly lovely today." She said, "I'd be even more flattered if I didn't think you said that to pretty much every woman that goes by." He responded with great charm, "I do say that a lot.") Just walking past that sign gave him great pleasure, such was its beauty. He found that for the rest of the day he couldn't stop thinking about it.

The next day when he left his house, that little voice inside his head said, "I'm actually kind of looking forward to seeing that sign." Sure enough, as he walked past the sign, Dr. B. felt that same surge of admiration he experienced the previous day. "This is a beautiful work of art!" he exclaimed to himself. This happened every day. He found himself eagerly anticipating walking past that sign and admiring its beauty, until one day the strangest thing happened. As he walked past that house and saw the sign, this time the voice inside of his head said to him, "Why should your neighbor have a sign as beautiful as that and not you? Think of how much joy it would give you to possess something of such beauty and have the whole neighborhood see it and know it belongs to you. You ought to have that. You must have that."

If that wasn't enough, another peculiar thing happened. Walking past his neighbor's house did not bring him joy anymore. Now it just troubled him. Now every time he saw that sign, it was a reminder of what he did not have and might never have. He knew it would be expensive to buy such a sign, and as a teacher, he did not make very much money. He and his wife were putting their children through school. Even if he had the money, he knew his wife would not want him to spend so much money on a sign.

He continued walking past that sign and feeling resentful that he could not have one like it until eventually one day he passed the sign and heard another voice inside his head. "Dr. B....," it began (even God calls him Dr. B.), "couldn't you enjoy that sign without owning it? Couldn't you be happy for the guy who has it? Couldn't you be happy that people get to see it? Couldn't you admire it without torturing yourself over how to possess it? You can admire without having to acquire."

> "Couldn't you admire that sign without torturing yourself over how to possess it? You can admire without having to acquire."

And that is what he did. He just agreed with that thought, and from that day forward he walked past that sign and said to himself, "I'll just admire without the need to acquire."

CONSTANT CRAVING

The biblical writers consistently found when they asked themselves, "How is my soul doing?" that their souls were never satisfied. They were constantly yearning after something. The Hebrew word for soul, *nephesh*, is repeatedly described as longing or wanting or desiring or striving. That's why the word *nephesh* is often in the Bible translated as mouth or stomach or throat.

The Hebrew way of conveying human experience is very concrete. The Bible talks about the soul being hungry or thirsty or hollow or empty, not satisfied. You read statements like these: "It's better to be satisfied with what the eye sees than to live with a craving *nephesh*, a craving soul, which we all have." The book of Genesis records a horribly violent story of a man named Shechem who violated a woman named Dinah. It says in effect, "His *nephesh*, his soul, craved Dinah."

When the will has become enslaved by its need, when the mind has become obsessed with the object of its desire, when the appetite of the body has become master rather than servant, the soul is disordered. The ultimate reality behind human dissatisfaction is sinful souls that have been cut off from the God we were made to rest in. That's why we're dissatisfied.

Our souls are always craving, never satisfied. The prophet Habakkuk wrote about sinful man: "See, the enemy is puffed up; his desires are not upright ... indeed, wine betrays him; he is arrogant and never at rest." This is life in our world, never at rest. He opens his soul up as wide as the grave "... and like death is never satisfied." Sometimes in the Old Testament the soul is pictured as a hollow place that is dominated by hunger; the soul craves the first-ripe figs or meat or wine.

A lot of people are dissatisfied with their jobs. "Theologian" Drew Carey said, "You hate your job? There's a support group for that. It's called everybody. They meet at the bar." A research group affiliated with the University of Chicago recently listed the ten least happy jobs in the world and the ten happiest jobs in the world. What they found was the ten least happy jobs actually were more financially lucrative and offered higher status than the ten happiest jobs. The difference? People in the happiest jobs had a higher sense of meaning. Less money, less status, but a higher sense of meaning. The main thing you bring home from your work is not a paycheck. The main thing you bring home from work is your soul. Work is a soul function. We're made to create value. The writer of Ecclesiastes says, "There is nothing better for a person than that he should make his soul enjoy good in his work. This too, I see, is from the hand of God."

A paradox of the soul is that it is incapable of satisfying itself, but it is also incapable of living without satisfaction. You were made for soul-satisfaction, but you will only ever find it in God. The soul craves to be secure. The soul craves to be loved. The soul craves to be significant, and we find these only in God in a form that can satisfy us. That's why the psalmist says to God, "Because your love is better than life … my soul will be satisfied as with the richest of foods." Soul and appetite and satisfaction are dominant themes in the Bible — the soul craves because it is meant for God. "My soul, find rest in God."

STRATEGIC DISAPPOINTMENT

Jesus said if you devote your life to pleasing yourself, you will actually destroy your soul, whereas if you place honoring God above pleasing yourself, then your soul will be truly satisfied. "For whoever wants to save their soul will lose it, but whoever loses their soul for me and the gospel will save it." The soul desires a life that is more than the satisfaction of desire. In other words, you will never achieve satisfaction if you make the goal of your life achieving satisfaction.

The psalmist echoes this paradox when he wrote, "My heart is not proud, O LORD. My eyes are not haughty … I have stilled and quieted my soul; like a weaned child with his mother, like a weaned child is my soul within me." This is a striking picture of my relationship with my soul. How do you wean a child? You do it by strategic disappointment. You deliberately withhold from the child what she wants so the child learns she can be master and not slave of her appetites.

This metaphor suggests your soul is becoming like that weaned child. It's not constantly troubling you with unsatisfied desires all the time. You are learning that your soul can be satisfied with God, even if all the appetites of your body or the desires floating around in your mind are not being gratified every moment because, in fact, gratification of mind and body will actually dismantle your soul.

Strategic disappointment is another of those categories where research reinforces soul wisdom. It turns out that even monkeys who receive mild stress in infancy, adolescence, and adulthood actually grow through it. They are better able to handle stressful situations; they are also more curious and explorative and resilient in the world in general. Also, mild stress seems to increase brain size, and actually causes brand-new neurons to develop. Whenever you're disappointed, whenever you don't get your way, take that disappointment as a chance to practice soul-satisfaction in God.

> Whenever you're disappointed, whenever you don't get your way, take that disappointment as a chance to practice soul-satisfaction in God.

That really works, as I sort of learned the hard way. Nancy and I met with a friend who happened to talk with someone we had both worked with at our former church in Chicago. He said that this individual had good things to say about both of us, so of course I wanted to know what he said, especially about me. My friend started with Nancy.

He went on and on about how Nancy lights up a room. That made sense, because she does. If you know her, you know this. She brings so much energy. She makes everybody else just come alive. She plays hard, and she laughs hard, and she goes deep, and she works hard. She says hard things nobody else in the room has the guts to say. She makes everybody else around her just want to be a better human being. It was nice to hear that our mutual friend remembered that about Nancy, but I still wanted to hear what he had said about me.

"John," he said, "you are admired for how you work within your limitations."

Initially, I was disappointed. That's not exactly what I wanted him to say. I was the monkey in the stress test and needed to grow through my disappointment, and in that moment I did. I got over myself and rested in the joy that Nancy was remembered so well. I allowed my soul to be satisfied by simply being loved by God.

That same week, I got some news from two friends of mine, both deeply involved in the same vocational field. One called to tell me he had gotten a big promotion. The other friend called to inform me that he was passed over for a promotion. Here's what's so cool about the appeal of a satisfied soul: My friend who didn't get the promotion threw a huge party to celebrate the good news for his friend who did. What a great example of a soul resting in God rather than depending on applause and achievement.

Here's some soul homework, by way of Dallas Willard:

> If you want to really experience the flow of love as never before, the next time you are in a competitive situation [around work or relationship or whose kids are the highest achieving or looks or whatever], pray that the others around you will be more outstanding, more praised, and more used of God than yourself. Really pull for them and rejoice in their success. If Christians were universally to do this for each other, the earth would soon be filled with the knowledge of the glory of God.

THE SOUL WORSHIPS WHAT IT DESIRES

I attended a funeral where the deceased was a man who used to joke when he was alive that he was a CEO church guy—Christmas and Easter Only. "My body will darken the door of a church just twice a year," he used to laugh. It was funny in a way until I thought, "Except the last year of your life. Then it will be Christmas, Easter, and a funeral." His church attendance increased by 50 percent in his last year.

The fact is, we satisfy our souls through worship.

Philosophy professor Kent Dunnington writes about a paramedic he knows who received an anonymous call that a heroin addict was near death in a nearby abandoned building. When the paramedic got there, the poor man was shivering in a corner, already unresponsive and near death. The apartment was foul-smelling and littered with trash and drug paraphernalia.

Kent asked his friend what it was like. The paramedic's comment was stunning: "It was terrifying, but for the first time in my life I understood what worship looks like."

Addiction, Kent explained, is a kind of worship, a kind of counterfeit worship. For the soul was created to worship. The soul requires a center to give it identity, to have a purpose for its activities, to give it a hope and a foundation. There is no such thing as an uncommitted person. An addict is the supreme example of trying to satisfy the soul with all the wrong things. The more it's fed, the more it craves. One of the ways to diagnose your ultimate commitment is to ask yourself: What do you get most irritated about when your soul is threatened?

Author and former seminary professor Neal Plantinga once said something amazing about our capacity for addiction. He said it shows that we were wired for ecstasy. Not the drug, but pure, ecstatic joy. Our ceaseless craving for more, though it can kill us when unredeemed, may be a hint of the joy that we were made for when the soul finds its center in God.

> The paradox of soul-satisfaction is this: When I die to myself, my soul comes alive.

The paradox of soul-satisfaction is this: When I die to myself, my soul comes alive. God says the wrong approach to soul thirst is through human achievement and material wealth. So soul-satisfaction is not about acquiring the right things but about acquiring the right soul. It is not something you buy, but something you receive freely from God.

Hear these great words of the prophet Isaiah: "Come, all you who are thirsty, come to the waters; and you who have no money, come, buy and eat! Come, buy wine and milk without money and without cost. Why spend money on what is not bread, and your labor on what does not satisfy? Listen, listen to me, and eat what is good, and [your soul] will delight in the richest of fare."

And it will be satisfied.

CHAPTER 15

THE SOUL NEEDS GRATITUDE

Try a little experiment. It will take all of two days, but it will teach you an important soul lesson.

Today, when you greet people, begin your conversation with a little complaint. The Bible calls that grumbling, as in "Do everything without grumbling." It might be a complaint about something in your life: your health, your job, money problems, the fact that you don't have a spouse, the fact that you *do* have the spouse that you have. It might be something about the person you're greeting. You don't like how they're dressed. Or you just don't like their personality, or maybe you're jealous. Just greet a friend or colleague with something like, "Man, did I have a horrible night's sleep." I'd be thrilled if you couldn't think of anything.

Tomorrow, try to greet people with a word of gratitude. I hope this is a lot easier for you than today's assignment. Think about something you're genuinely grateful for: your family, a friend, your health, your job, the weather, your church. It might sound something like this: "Wow, on a morning like this, it just feels good to be alive, doesn't it?"

After you try this little experiment, ask yourself which day produced more positive feelings in you. Which day left you feeling vibrant, more alive, and closer to God? I'm pretty sure I know the answer because the soul thrives on gratitude. We feel better when we are grateful because the fundamental mind-set of the life of the soul is gratitude.

In Paul's letter to the church at Colossae, he offered some new rules to help them live more authentically as followers of Christ. False teaching had introduced heresy into the church, and Paul wanted to remind them to practice the very attitude of Jesus as they interacted with each other and their neighbors. After listing such qualities as compassion, kindness, patience, humility, and the like, he ends this section of his letter with an appeal for gratitude: "And be thankful.... sing psalms, hymns, and spiritual songs with gratitude in your hearts to God. And whatever you do, whether in word or in deed, do it all in the name of the Lord Jesus, giving thanks to God through him."

In another of his letters, he exhorts Christians to "give thanks in all circumstances, for this is God's will for you in Christ Jesus."

The truth is, all of us can get so caught up in ourselves that we too often don't take the time to be grateful — to God and to others.

Remember, these people had been redeemed by God — followers of Jesus — yet they needed to be reminded to be grateful. Not just when things went well, but in *all* circumstances. If anyone would practice gratitude, shouldn't it be Christians? The truth is, all of us can get so caught up in ourselves that we too often don't take the time to be grateful — to God and to others. "Why, my soul, are you downcast?" the psalmist asks. Maybe it's because you are not feeding it with the gratitude it needs.

GOD'S BENEFIT PACKAGE

More gratitude will not come from acquiring more things or experiences, but from more of an awareness of God's presence and his goodness. It's a way of looking at life, always perceiving the good. Gratitude is a by-product of a way of seeing things, and it always involves three factors. The language is a little unusual, so you will just have to bear with it. It comes from the old Latin word *bene*, which meant good, and gratitude will always involve three *benes*.

First, the *benefit*. In order to be grateful, you have to receive and recognize a gift that you believe is good. You find it favorable. The Bible says, "Praise the LORD, my soul ... and forget not all his benefits—who forgives all your sins and heals all your diseases, who redeems your life from the pit and crowns you with love and compassion, who satisfies your desires with good things ..." It doesn't get any better than that, does it? But the important thing to remember is that God does all this. These are the benefits he gives us, and the soul responds with gratitude.

Second, gratitude requires that there be a *benefactor*. Again the little word *bene*, Latin for "good," this time coupled with factor, which is related to the word *factory*. A benefactor is one who does good, a little factory that produces good. To be truly grateful you must not only recognize the benefits or gifts that come your way, but that they are not just random acts; they are not accidents. They are coming from Someone who has good intentions for you. To be grateful as a Christian, you must believe that the good that is in your life comes from God. Not from your own efforts or merit. Not from others who might want to impress or manipulate you for their gain.

The apostle James writes, "Don't be deceived, my dear brothers and sisters. Every good and perfect gift is from above, coming down from the Father of the heavenly lights...." Light is an expression of goodness, and when we consider what he has done for us and what he has given us, our souls are grateful.

In addition to the benefit and the benefactor, there is the *beneficiary*: the one who receives the good gifts of God. And that's you. You are the beneficiary of the benefits of a God who has your best interests at heart, and this is going on all the time. When we take that for granted or believe we deserve his gifts, then we are no longer grateful; you can't be grateful for something you believe you are entitled to, and without a grateful heart the soul suffers. Because the soul needs gratitude.

This is where many of us fail the gratitude test, because we tend to look around us and believe all that we have was gained by our own resourcefulness. Or that we're entitled to the blessings in our lives. But gratitude always comes from a posture of humility. When you buy a new car and drive it home from the showroom, you may be thrilled that you can buy a new car, but you're not necessarily grateful to GM or Ford. But what if I drove a brand-new Porsche to your home, pulled into the driveway, and handed you the keys? "Here — it's yours. I just want you to have this." I'm pretty sure you'd at least say, "Thank you."

Am I kidding? You'd probably hug me and thank me and ask me why in the world I did this and hug me again and thank me over and over. You would have a hard time believing your good fortune. That's the kind of gratitude our soul needs as we consider all that God has done for us. All that we have been given that we don't deserve.

The default mode of the sinful human race is entitlement, the belief that this gift or that experience that God placed in my path is rightfully mine. I am owed.

Here's the deal: The more you think you're entitled to, the less you will be grateful for. The bigger the sense of entitlement, the smaller the sense of gratitude. We wonder why in our world we keep getting more and more and more and keep being less and less and less grateful. This is precisely why.

My sinful mind can convince me that anything I want I'm entitled to, and if I'm not getting something I want, somebody in the universe must be messing up, and they owe me, and they ought to pay for it. In fact, this has led to a proliferation of lawsuits, because when we don't get something we really want, we want to sue somebody.

I'm not a boat guy, but I have friends who know boats. They tell me choosing a name for a boat is a really big deal. When I was in college, one of my instructors was dean over his department. He had a fishing boat he loved. He actually named his boat *Faculty Development* so he could write on his staff report, "I'm spending more and more time on faculty development." And this was at a Christian college, believe it or not.

My former colleague Bill Hybels once saw in the Newport Beach harbor in California a beautiful, gleaming, million-dollar yacht whose name was painted in big, bold letters across it. Its name was *Deserved*. Whatever I have, I deserve. Entitlement grows deep within us. This is why, for the soul, ingratitude is not just a psychological problem. It's not just an impoverishment of our emotional experience. It's a sin.

> *Entitlement grows deep within us. This is why, for the soul, ingratitude is not just a psychological problem or an impoverishment of our emotional experience. It's a sin.*

Paul says it's the hallmark of a life opposed to God. "For although they knew God, they neither glorified him as God nor gave thanks to him, but their thinking became futile ..." This connection is so interesting. Their thinking was futile. They perceived themselves to be entitled, to be owed, not as grateful receivers of grace every moment. "... forget not all his benefits ..."

TRAINING FOR GRATITUDE

In Jesus' day, every devout Israelite would pray what was called The Eighteen Benedictions. There's that root word again, *bene*: good. Plus *diction*: words, speech. A benediction was good words. In Hebrew, a benediction was any prayer that began with the word *bless*. In the morning when they woke up, they would pray eighteen times, "Blessed are you, God." At night before they went to bed, they would pray eighteen times, "Blessed are you, God." In the middle of the day, they would pause and pray the eighteen, "Blessed are you, Lord, who abundantly forgives." The Hebrew benedictions connected the gift with the Giver. It reminded the citizens of Israel that all that was good came from God.

They were training for gratitude, and they loved doing this, because they knew life with God was the good life. They would pray the eighteen an extra time on the Sabbath because they loved the Sabbath so much. They fully knew who provided the good life, and their souls were grateful.

The Hebrew term for gratitude is *hikarat hatov,* which means, literally, "recognizing the good." That's what sustains your soul. That's what lifts you beyond yourself and into God's presence. I began this chapter with an experiment, and I would like to close it with two more. Consider these experiments "gratitude training."

The first one is to write what I call the "gratitude letter." It works like this: Think of somebody who has impacted your life for the good, somebody maybe whom you've known for quite a while: a friend, a mentor, an encourager. Somebody without whom you'd be a different person. Then take the time to write them a letter telling why you are grateful to God for them. It doesn't have to be a term paper—aim for around something between a Twitter post (140 characters) and a couple of pages. Don't worry about making it grammatically perfect or a work of literary art. Just tell that person why you are grateful for them. I've found that the discipline of putting your thoughts like this on paper helps you—and the other person—see just why you are so grateful for them.

After you write your "gratitude letter," try to meet with that person face-to-face. You might need to practice a little sanctified deception—don't tell them why you want to meet, or you might scare them off: "Haven't seen you for a while—let's meet for coffee." Then when you get there, pull out that letter and read it to them word for word. "This is why I'm grateful to God for you." You might want to have a copy to give to them. If this sounds like it might be an awkward experience, it's because we seldom take the time to deliberately express our gratitude to each other. And that's a shame, because it is one of the best things you can do for your own soul as well as the souls of others. I am not much for guarantees, but I think I can say with certainty that writing and then reading your gratitude letter will lift your soul in a remarkable and unforgettable way.

The next gratitude experiment is to pray your own benedictions

—brief statements that recognize the good that comes from God. You don't have to start with eighteen. That might be overwhelming. The best way to do this is to first make a list of all that you are truly grateful to God for providing. Then go back through this list and begin with the words, "Blessed are you, O Lord."

- Blessed are you, O Lord, for giving me my children.
- Blessed are you, O Lord, who gave me life and good health today.
- Blessed are you, O Lord, for helping me get through this difficult day.
- Blessed are you, O Lord, who forgives me when I sin.
- Blessed are you, O Lord, for the great sunset you let me enjoy.

Is it really necessary to use those words, "Blessed are you"? While the point of this exercise is to feed your soul with gratitude, there really *is* something special about these words that is worth considering. To bless someone means to offer happiness or praise to them. When you say "Blessed are you, O Lord," you are not only expressing gratitude, but you are saying, "I want to make you happy and praise you, God, with my gratitude for what you have done." It's a subtle reminder that gratitude is good for both the person expressing it and the one receiving it.

I recently had one of those mornings when I just didn't want to wake up. A pile of unresolved problems and a weariness of soul made rolling over and grabbing another hour of rest appealing. But then I began practicing gratitude. I mentally walked through the previous day in a grateful state of mind:

I got to exercise, and I love having a body with enough strength and energy to exercise. What a gift that is. Not everyone has it.

I got to learn. I love learning. I even get paid to learn. How cool is that?

I'm married to a beautiful and gifted woman. We have three adult children, and they are doing well.

I got to travel someplace. People in other centuries never got to do this kind of thing, and they would have given anything to do so, and I can just get in my car and go wherever I want to go.

By the time I finished reviewing yesterday, I thought, "Wow, I got to live this day. Are you kidding me? I got to do that? And today I get to live another day?"

You will not always feel grateful. But you can take the time each day to remember the benefits you received, see your benefactor, and thank him for his benefits.

There was only one thing to say. "Thank you, God!"

It doesn't always happen that way. Gratitude does not always come naturally. You will not always *feel* grateful. But you can take the time each day to remember the benefits you received, see your benefactor, and thank him for his benefits.

As Thornton Wilder put it, "We can only be said to be alive in those moments when our hearts are conscious of our treasures."

PART 3

THE SOUL RESTORED

CHAPTER 16

DARK NIGHT
OF THE SOUL

If you ask people who don't believe in God why they don't, the number one reason will be suffering. If you ask people who believe in God when they grew most spiritually, the number one answer will be suffering.

My father-in-law, Al, had been in the non-believer category since he was a boy and had been badly hurt by the church. His family was very poor; in desperation his mother went to the church for help and came home in tears, empty-handed. It was one of the only times he saw her cry. He would not open up his heart to a God who would make his mother cry.

When his only daughter married a preacher, he wasn't opposed to my occupation, mostly just removed. He was a hunting/fishing/sportsman kind of guy. Nancy was their only child, and one of the pictures of her I love the most has her cradling a shotgun in her arms. She was four years old at the time. When our first two children were born—both girls—Al was gaga about them. He taught our eldest to know what sound a birdie makes: "Bang." Just to get her ready for her first shotgun. But the third time around we had a boy, and Al had been waiting for one of those a long time.

That same year, in the space of a few days, Al's skin turned the color of a ripe banana. It was cancer—a very dire kind. He lived through a year and a half of physical pain and bodily humiliation.

But his heart opened up to God. We began to pray and read the Bible together. In his last conversation with Nancy, he told her how much he loved her. He died the day after Valentine's Day, the day before his wedding anniversary, after a year of more peace than he had ever known. The darkest year of his life became, somehow, the year of light.

The darkest year of his life became, somehow, the year of light.

During the early days of our marriage, I also came to know a friend, Gary Moon. I met Gary, a red-haired Georgia boy with a deep Southern drawl, when we both entered a clinical psychology program in California. We ended up in a supervisory group together. I don't remember any supervision at all, but I do remember lying on the ground and laughing at Gary's stories.

Gary was from a small sect called the Pentecostal Holiness Church that was incapable of being uninteresting. His Uncle Otis was a faith healer with a knack for memorable lines. He once asked a demon-possessed man to reveal his identity. "Liar," the demon responded. Uncle Otis immediately asked, "Are you telling me the truth, lying demon?" thus effectively putting the minion of darkness into an inescapable double-bind. Uncle Otis also prayed over a man who told him that he suffered from constipation: "Lord, heal this man *immediately!*" — a prayer that went mercifully unanswered. These were the stories that Gary would tell during our months of clinical work together.

For many years after we graduated, Gary and I were in only sporadic contact, seeing each other periodically at psychology conventions. He had returned to Georgia while I stayed in California. In time, just as both of us had been drawn to the same school to study theology and psychology, we were both drawn to the work of Dallas Willard. Gary edited a journal on Dallas's writings and asked me to contribute a paper to the journal.

Eventually a college in Santa Barbara, California, called Westmont formed the Dallas Willard Center for Spiritual Formation. Gary and his wife, Regina, moved so Gary could serve as executive director; I became a member of the board.

One August afternoon in 2012, as I was working on this book, I joined Gary for lunch. "How's Dallas?" I asked. Dallas had been experiencing some health difficulties over the summer; I had talked with him a few days earlier and knew that Gary had just come back from visiting him and Jane.

"How good are you at compartmentalizing?" Gary asked. "I'd rather not talk about it on a golf course." I died a little inside.

We waited until dinner, sitting on a deck watching the sun go down beyond the Channel Islands, framed by the beauty of Santa Barbara's harbor and palm-lined beachfront.

"It's cancer," Gary said. It was the same kind of cancer that my wife's father had died from twenty-three years earlier.

WHEN GOD SEEMS SILENT

Because the soul is the deepest expression of the person, the soul is the place of greatest pain. We do not speak of the dark night of the mind, or the will, or even the spirit. Only the soul. The dark night of the soul.

The phrase comes from a brilliant Carmelite monk named John who lived in Spain in the sixteenth century. He devoted his life to reforming the church, but his attempts were heavily criticized, and he ended up in prison. It was there in confinement, with his dreams lost, that he wrote his most famous work: *The Dark Night of the Soul*. It is an account of how God works to change us not just through joy and light, but through confusion, through disappointment, through loss. Because of his commitment in the midst of suffering, he became known as "St. John of the Cross."

The dark night of the soul, as he described it, is not simply the experience of suffering. It is suffering in what feels like the silence of God.

This saint who bore the name of the cross of Jesus said that in the early days of spiritual life, the soul often finds delight in devotional activities: We love to read the Bible, we hunger for worship, we long to pray. We may think this is a sign of our maturity; it is really more a kind of honeymoon phase.

"But there will come a time when God will bid them to grow deeper. He will remove the previous consolation of the soul in order to teach it virtue...." In the dark night, my prayers feel like they reach no higher than the ceiling. (Although, Dallas often said, if we truly understand how radically present God is in our world, reaching the ceiling is more than high enough.) In the dark night, the Bible I read turns to ashes. In the dark night, words and books and songs that once spoke to my soul now leave me cold.

It is important to understand that the dark night, as John writes about it, is not the soul's fault. Of course, it's possible for me to grow cold toward God because I cling to sin, or prefer an idol, or simply become lazy. These are all real occurrences that require wise response. But they are not the dark night. The dark night is God-initiated.

There's an old illustration that was used to teach uninterrupted intimacy with God as the norm for successful spiritual life. It never failed to add guilt to spiritual dryness. It is a picture of intimacy with God that's as old as bench seats in the front of cars. A husband and wife are driving together. She says to him: "When we were dating, we used to sit next to each other while we drove; you would have your arm around me, I would lay my head on your shoulder, and I felt so loved. Now look at the distance between us." And the husband replies: "Who moved?"

In the dark night of the soul, it is God who moved.

God may still be in the car. But he's scrunched up small and pressing hard against the passenger door. I stretch my arm but I can't reach him or feel him or touch him. My soul has not changed seats. God moved.

WAITING IN THE DARK

The practices that once fed my soul feed it no more. John of the Cross, writing from his prison cell, says in the dark night the soul is pained but not hopeless. "God's love is not content to leave us in our weakness, and for this reason he takes us into a dark night. He weans us from all of the pleasures by giving us dry times and inward darkness.... No soul will ever grow deep in the spiritual life unless God works passively in that soul by means of the dark night." We have a hard time with the dark night. Our churches are practical places, and we generally tell people the answer to any spiritual problem is more: more prayer, more serving, more giving, more trying.

But John says just the opposite. When the soul begins to enjoy the benefits of the spiritual life and then has them taken away, it becomes embittered and angry. There are some who become angry at themselves at this point, thinking that their loss of joy is a result of something they have done or have neglected to do. They will fuss and fret and do all they can to recover this consolation. They will strive to become saints in a day. They will make all kinds of resolutions to be more spiritual, but the greater the resolution, the greater the fall.

Their problem is that they lack the patience that waits for whatever God would give them and when God chooses to give. They must learn spiritual meekness, which will come about in the dark night.

What do we do in the dark night?

We do nothing. We wait. We remember that we are not God. We hold on. We ask for help. We do less. We resign from things, we rest more, we stop going to church, we ask somebody else to pray because we can't. We let go of our need to hurry through it.

They lack the patience that waits for whatever God would give them and when God chooses to give. They must learn spiritual meekness, which will come about in the dark night.

You can't run in the dark.

We love psalms about restoring our souls. They are sometimes called psalms of orientation—psalms that help us direct our lives to God. But there are other psalms. After we learned of Dallas's diagnosis, my wife delivered a message based on what Walter Brueggemann calls "psalms of disorientation." These are the psalms where the soul is disoriented; God is absent; darkness is winning. "Break the teeth in their mouths, O God.... Let them vanish like water that flows away ... like a slug that melts away as it moves along, like a stillborn child that never sees the sun." That's one that doesn't get used at a lot of prayer breakfasts. Eugene Peterson once wrote that before we can love our enemies, we have to pray our hatred. In these psalms — which are more frequent than the psalms of orientation — Israel vented and boiled over at God, apparently believing he was secure enough to be able to take it.

Nancy talked about an unmarried friend who once punctured the polite piety of a small group Bible study that was having an abstract discussion about "where is God when it hurts?" With the honesty rarely seen in Bible study groups, she declared, "If Jesus thinks that three hours on a cross makes up for forty-two years of singleness, I think that's crazy."

Cool!

Nancy waited for the group to get swallowed up in a sinkhole. Eventually someone chirped in with a Christian cliché, and the moment passed. But there was more honest faith in that one real comment than all the safe platitudes that came before and after it.

In my own darkest time some years ago, my greatest disappointment was deep and unfixable. I questioned my calling. I didn't think about suicide, but I definitely thought that if my life were over, I'd be grateful for the end of pain. I would talk to a few close friends, and they would generally give sympathy and support, for which I was grateful.

But then I did what I have so often done when I cannot think or pray or reason my way out of something. I called Dallas. I walked him through the circumstances and the heartbreak and the pain, eager for his answer.

Long pause.

"This will be a test of your joyful confidence in God."

Silence.

I did not miss the challenge in this sentence, all the more goading for its gentle phrasing. Not just my confidence — my joyful confidence. Human beings around the globe had been suffering a year ago, and I was capable of joy then. Why should I consider my own suffering grounds for a crisis of confidence in God when I don't react the same way to others?

If there is a God who is worthy to be the Father of Jesus, I can trust giving this situation as well as my own feelings joyfully into his hands. If there is not, I have infinitely bigger problems than a merely human circumstance. Either way it is true: this will be a test of my joyful confidence in God.

AWED BY THE SLOWNESS OF GOD

Modern churches with linear models of spiritual growth and large-scale models for devotional life rarely speak of or help people with the dark night. We are uncomfortable with it because we want to do something—because we sell formulas and steps and programs, and the dark night of the soul is not our program. The dark night is for souls that learn to wait.

After Gary told me about Dallas's diagnosis that August, I drove back to Box Canyon to talk and pray with Dallas and Jane. They began to receive notes and prayers from people all around the world. In particular, they began to hear from people who also journey in the night.

Joni Eareckson Tada, who has spent her adult life paralyzed and in a wheelchair, and more recently has written of her own struggle with cancer, heard about Dallas and sent to him and Jane these words from a nineteenth-century writer named Frederick Faber:

> In the spiritual life God chooses to try our patience first of all by His slowness. He is slow: we are swift and precipitate. It is because we are but for a time, and He has been for eternity.... There is something greatly overawing in the extreme slowness of God. Let it overshadow our souls, but let it not disquiet them. We must wait for God, long, meekly, in the wind and wet, in the thunder and the lightning, in the cold and the dark. Wait, and He will come. He never comes to those who do not wait. He does not go their road. When He comes, go with Him, but go slowly, fall a little behind; when he quickens

His pace, be sure of it, before you quicken yours. But when He slackens, slacken at once: and do not be slow only, but silent, very silent, for He is God.

When I read that, I was reminded of Dallas's own words to me: "You must ruthlessly eliminate hurry from your life."

Dallas and Jane showed me a little book they got from Dieter Zander, *A Stroke of Grace*. Dieter and I had worked together in Chicago at Willow Creek Community Church; he was an artist, musician, and teacher. Willow Creek was at the time perhaps the highest-profile church in the country, and Dieter was its highest-profile worship leader. He led worship with so much vigor that at times he (literally) left blood on the keyboard from cracked fingernails. He led with such energy that we actually had to stop doing certain songs because people in the balconies jumped around too much and the facilities engineers were afraid the whole thing would come down — a kind of joy-driven variation of Samson and the Philistines.

Dieter loved the writings of Henri Nouwen, a Dutch-born Catholic priest and prolific author. I remember having a long discussion with him about Nouwen's reflections on a verse in the gospel of John. Jesus told Peter that as a young man, Peter had gone where he wanted, but when he was old, Peter would be dressed by other hands and led to where he did not want to go. We were young men then; the vulnerability of aging was poignant to us.

There is something greatly overawing in the extreme slowness of God. Let it overshadow our souls, but let it not disquiet them. We must wait for God.

FREDERICK FABER

One night when Dieter was in his late forties, he began to shake violently. He suffered a massive stroke in the left hemisphere of his brain. When he awoke six days later, he was no longer able to communicate as he had; he had to learn to say his wife's name, to say his sons' names. He could no longer use his right hand and therefore he could no longer lead worship. The music and words that flowed out of him were now mostly trapped in his brain.

He used to work on a stage, before thousands of people who applauded his every move. Now he works in a windowless room in the back of a Trader Joe's grocery store. He breaks down boxes. When fruit is bruised, if a pear falls on the floor—when any product is no longer regarded as perfect, it is brought to Dieter. From him it will go to feed the hungry, who do not care if their apple is lopsided.

Dieter once wrote in a letter:

It is good that I work there. I am like that fruit. I am imperfect. Inside I am the same person, the same sense of humor, the same thoughts. But my words betray me. What should take three minutes to say is an hour of frustration. People lose patience with me. Aphasia means aloneness. But God hears me. My world is small, and quiet, and slow and simple. No stage. No performance. More real. Good.

A year or so after Dieter's stroke, he and his wife, Val, visited Nancy and me. He used a small whiteboard to help him communicate. Toward the end of our time together, he began to write a Bible verse. I knew which one it would be even before he scribbled it on the board: John 21:18: "When you were younger you dressed yourself and went where you wanted; but when you are old you will stretch out your hands, and someone else will dress you and lead you where you do not want to go." Then below that verse, Dieter wrote: "Good."

> "Whatever my lot, Thou has taught me to say,
> 'It is well, it is well with my soul.' "

KEEP ETERNITY BEFORE THE CHILDREN

Dallas had to go through an operation called the "Whipple procedure," a brutal invasion of the body that my wife (who was a nurse, and who watched her dad go through this) always describes inelegantly as having the doctor gut you like a fish. It's not a risk-free operation. When we gathered to pray for him, Dallas said before going through it, "Whatever happens will be wonderful."

Watching Dallas walk this path was like watching a scout, who has been doing advance work anyway, begin to walk into a country where we will all one day arrive. He said once, "I think that, when I die, it may take some time before I know it."

Huh?

A person, Dallas said, is essentially a collection of conscious experiences. Far more than just bodies or just appetites, we are our experiences. That's why we treasure the good ones so — a beautiful sunset, a favorite scene in a movie, a first kiss, a dramatic victory.

> *A person is essentially a collection of conscious experiences. Far more than just bodies or just appetites, we are our experiences. That's why we treasure the good ones.*
> **DALLAS WILLARD**

This conscious experience of life, Dallas said, will go right on uninterrupted by death. Jesus put it so strikingly: "The one who trusts in me will never taste death." What does it mean to never taste death? Why did he say it like that?

My friend Gary said that the phrase that came to his mind, watching Dallas walk in the valley of the shadow of death, was "Game on."

The shadow had found a worthy adversary.

CHAPTER 17

MORNING

We have this hope as an anchor of the soul, firm and secure.

HEBREWS 6:19

The soul is a ship that needs an anchor.

I am sitting once more in the living room in Box Canyon, the one I had met Dallas in decades earlier. Not much has changed in the room. The furniture is the same. The air conditioner roars; Jane says they probably should get a new one but the old one keeps working. I look at Dallas — now my hair is grayer than his was when we first met. My children are grown. I have been able to write books and speak and do many things that I would have been glad to know about when I was in this room the first time. And I have failed and been disappointed in ways that would have seemed unbearable then.

He is wearing an old bathrobe. When we were cleaning out the garage, he found a few old Bibles from many decades ago. They are falling apart from age and use, underlined and scribbled in, and he greets them as if he is visiting treasured companions after a long absence. We found a scythe in the garage that Dallas used to clear weeds when he was a young boy in Missouri; his father used it before him and his father's father before that; it is his heirloom.

I marvel at his peace.

WHAT REALLY MATTERS

A few of us gather around him to pray. Dallas begins to sing, still leading worship as he did when he was a preacher boy in his teens, and we join in. What matters is the work, Dallas tells us. What matters is the work of helping people know that God is alive and present and loves them; that this reality that Jesus called the kingdom is among us and available; and that life is precious, yet is wasted with terrible ease. I think, as I watch his emaciated body and hear his vision, of how devotion to movements must be formed in times like these around one who can inspire so.

We all have two worlds, an outer world that is visible and public and obvious, and an inner world that may be chaotic and dark or may be gloriously beautiful. In the end, the outer world fades. We are left with the inner world. It is what we will take with us. I am an unceasing spiritual being with an eternal destiny in God's glorious universe.

"Do you regret anything?" someone asked him.

"I regret the time I have wasted," he answered.

Huh?

If there is any human being on the planet who has not wasted time, it is Dallas. I don't think he'd know what a television was if one hit him on the head. He is either reading or teaching or doing ministry. Or doing bits of carpentry around their place in Box Canyon, or mentoring students, or praying. If Dallas is guilty of wasting time, the rest of us may as well sign up for vagrancy hell right now.

But I think, maybe, this time I know what he means. "[Redeem] the time," the apostle Paul said, "because the days are evil." The language is exactly right, I heard Dallas say once. The reason our souls hunger so is that the life we could be living so far exceeds our strangest dreams. I had a friend once who knew when still a young man that he was going to die of cancer, except that the hospital made a mistake that happens only in movies. They told him he wasn't going to die; he was going to live. And for an hour, for a day, he experienced a euphoria of gratitude beyond words. For those few hours, he got it right.

I think Dallas said he regretted all the time he wasted, not because he compared himself to other more efficient people, but because he began to see what life could be.

I remember a phrase I had heard from him years ago, about how all of us lost souls allow ourselves to live in worry and anger and self-importance and pettiness when life with God is all around us: Your time is already in the pawn shop of lost souls.

I think Dallas wanted his time back.

I watched him and thought of what a redeemed soul can be:

I think Dallas said he regretted all the time he wasted, not because he compared himself to other more efficient people, but because he began to see what life could be.

- To be able to say yes or no without anxiety or duplicity
- To speak with confidence and honesty
- To be willing to disappoint anybody, yet ready to bless everybody
- To have a mind filled with more noble thoughts than could ever be spoken
- To share without thinking
- To see without judging
- To be so genuinely humble that each person I see would be an object of wonder
- To love God

A LITTLE SLICE OF HEAVEN

The gospel, Dallas said once, means that this universe is a perfectly safe place for you to be.

Huh?

It means that the soul is simply not at risk. Not even from cancer. What else could Paul have meant when he said nothing can separate us from the love of God? Why else would Jesus have advised us not to worry?

Nancy and I hug Dallas and Jane. Nancy promises to send a special recipe for corn bread and biscuits that Dallas will be allowed to eat—he is diabetic now. I smiled at this quiet act of defiance. The chemotherapy and other treatments may limit his diet but have no power over his hunger for foods a Missouri boy grew up on.

Dallas sits in that house in Box Canyon and waits while his body goes through the slow death of chemo, and a little slice of heaven beams through that home, as it does through the most unlikely houses and huts and hovels around the planet.

People visit. People call. People write.

"We're praying for you."

The life of the village depends on the health of the stream.

The stream is your soul. And you are the Keeper.

EPILOGUE

Early on the morning of May 8, 2013, I got a phone call from Gary Black, a friend of Dallas and the family, telling me that Dallas Willard had died.

My first thought was to remember what Dallas had said about how when he died he wondered if it would be awhile before he realized it. I wonder if anyone's told him?

I remembered the death of my father-in-law from pancreatic cancer. What an unpleasant way of death it is. Dallas was unfailingly kind and patient with those who cared for him in the end; it would have been hard to imagine him otherwise.

Gary actually taped his conversation with Dallas during those final hours—What are you seeing? What is taking place?—as Dallas began what he spoke of as "the great transition." I have never heard a recording like it. It's like a conversation with a person who is about to cross over into a room that you cannot see and where you cannot go.

Gary said that Dallas's final words, in the midst of what was surely significant suffering, were, "Thank you. Thank you."

Gary was the only person in the room at the time, but he said that Dallas was not talking to him.

I'm not sure if anyone has told Dallas yet about his death, but it took three services here to say good-bye. One of them was at the little church he and Jane are a part of; a small service for family and friends. Another was a more public event at a larger venue. A third service was held at the school where Dallas has taught for almost five decades.

At all of them the same observations were made of a life lived with such humility and wisdom and readiness-to-serve. All of them ask the same question, though not in so many words: "How did such a life happen?"

Six months later, Nancy and I have lunch with a young couple. The husband had met Dallas a couple of times and had read his books. Even though they had only spoken a few times, this husband's life was somehow changed by this one acquaintance. We are part of a secret society, friends of a common friend.

The wife of this couple was pregnant: "Do you know if it's a boy or girl?"

"Boy."

"Have you picked out a name yet?"

"Yes. We're going to call him Dallas."

Life goes on. The world spins out another day. The mystery of human life and hope goes on. And here and there, the luminous light that shone out from a carpenter in Nazareth glimmers and flickers in the darkness. And we hope again for what life might become.

The soul waits.

ACKNOWLEDGMENTS

A book is a soulish thing. It is physical—dots of ink and paper from old trees—and yet it feeds our minds and moves our wills. We read with our bodies; with our wills we choose to have our thoughts guided by the words of another person. Books connect us with ourselves and with others—and perhaps with God.

This has been a book of particularly deep connections for me. I am grateful to my editor, John Sloan, and to our partner, Lyn Cryderman, for effort and contributions that have gone far beyond what is normally associated with an editor. Without Lyn's diligence, this book simply could not have happened. And it marks a milestone with a team of folks from Zondervan across the years who have been a family of support and nurture, for whom I will always be grateful.

Gary Moon is a treasured friend who has been generous with his thoughts and wisdom, and also made available the background about Dallas Willard's life and thought. Mark Nelson and Tremper Longman III are two scholars from Westmont College who provided helpful resources from the fields of philosophy and Old Testament studies. Agents Sealy and Curtis Yates are a joy to work with. Glenn Lucke and the Docent team provided research that was amazingly comprehensive and deep. I am enormously grateful to the church I serve, Menlo Park Presbyterian Church, for making it possible to have time to write and for the opportunity to work with Linda Barker, who helps make life and ministry possible in a thousand joyful ways. Rick Blackmon and Brad Wright and the SoulPulse team have helped flesh out what the "with God" life looks like. Patty and Eff Martin have helped make the dream of the Willard Center a reality, and its contributions are only beginning. Jane Willard and Becky Willard Heatley are fellow board members from whom I have learned much.

Laura Kathleen Ortberg Turner was a constant source of suggestion and encouragement. My wife, Nancy, is a treasure of energy and feedback and attitude and companionship that is a part of every word and thought.

For Dallas, I am one of countless people who find it impossible to express in words the nature or magnitude of the debt owed. His thinking has shaped me far more than anyone else's thinking, and his life has shaped me far more than his thinking. "Let no debt remain outstanding," the apostle Paul wrote, "except the continuing debt to love one another." It is a debt that I will joyfully and gratefully be unable to repay as long as I live.

BIBLE VERSIONS

SOURCES

Prologue

13: *Keeper of the Stream:* This is a version of a story told by Peter Marshall in a sermon. Beyond his story, there was a book written in 1952 called *Keeper of the Stream* about a man named Frank Sawyer who worked to beautify the river Avon. He died on the river Avon, an old man, in 1980.

Introduction

17: I have been to Box Canyon many times; some of these historical details are from Tracey Kaplan, "Once-Remote Box Canyon Being Pried Open," *Los Angeles Times* (March 19, 1989).

23: *private world:* Gordon MacDonald, *Ordering Your Private World* (Nashville: Thomas Nelson, 1984). More about this in Chapter 8.

CHAPTER 1: The Soul Nobody Knows

27: *"Most people, at most times":* Mark Baker and Stewart Goetz, *The Soul Hypothesis* (New York: Continuum Books, 2011), 100.

27: *It's the word that won't go away:* One of the primary reasons that the word *soul* is used less and less is the unpopularity of "dualism." The word *dualism* itself is loaded and complex; in one paper N. T. Wright lists ten different forms of dualism from theological to eschatological to moral and beyond. (http://ntwrightpage.com/Wright_SCP_MindSpiritSoulBody.htm)

Belief in the soul is generally associated with "substance dualism," the notion that spiritual — or unembodied personal power — actually exists and can be a causal force in our world.

One of the most common objections to dualism in contemporary (and much Christian) thought is that it often includes the idea (frequently associated with Plato) that matter is inferior to the realm of the spirit, and this leads to a devaluing of the body or of sexuality in ways that contradict the goodness of God's creation. Any form of dualism that fails to uphold the goodness of matter as God-created would fall short of biblical thought.

Another objection is that dualism seems increasingly unlikely as science (especially neuroscience) continues to tell us more about the workings of the human body (particularly the brain).

For the purposes of this book, my main concern is with those views of human life that argue that human beings are "nothing but" jiggling atoms or tissues and nerve endings (a view sometimes called "nothing buttery," and more often called "reductionism" because of the claim that understanding and explaining human existence can be reduced to the level of biology or chemistry). I think the most important aspect of "soul language" is that it affirms human beings as moral agents, with the capacity for free choice and therefore accountability, who will be resurrected by God and therefore are created for an eternal existence in his great universe. Christian thinkers such as Nancey Murphy, who advocates what she calls "non-reductionist materialism," would not tend to use the word soul and would disagree with dualism, but would still hold to this robust view of personhood that is part of classical Christianity. (For her view, see *Whatever Happened to the Soul?* Edited by Warren Brown, Nancey Murphy, and H. Newton Malony [Minneapolis: Fortress Press, 1998]).

For contemporary defenses of the traditional notion of the soul and of dualism, see Richard Swinburne, *The Evolution of the Soul* (New York: Oxford University Press, 1997), or John Cooper's excellent *Body, Soul, and Life Everlasting* (Grand Rapids: Eerdmans, 2000). I find their arguments compelling. Clearly, simply being a theist commits one to some form of dualism (God himself does not have a body). I'm not sure that trying to maintain a non-reductionist view of personhood in a cosmos created by an immaterial God will buy much extra scientific credibility with those who are skeptical about dualism in general.

28: Anne Lamott, *Help, Thanks, Wow: The Three Essential Prayers* (New York: Riverhead Books, 2012), 20.

28: *"If Daffy Duck were"*: Jeffrey Boyd, *Soul Psychology* (Colorado Springs: Soul Research Institute, 1994), 59.

29: *Soul weighs twenty-one grams*: Les Parrott, *You're Stronger Than You Think* (Carol Stream, IL: Tyndale, 2012), 116.

29: Owen Flanagan: Baker and Goetz, *The Soul Hypothesis*, 100.

29: *Patricia*: Boyd, *Soul Psychology*, 203ff.

30: *"The only thing I can depend on"*: Ibid., 203.

30: W.E.B Du Bois, *The Souls of Black Folk* (reprint, Healdburg, CA: Eucalyptus Press, 2013).

31: William Pollard, *The Soul of the Firm* (Grand Rapids: Zondervan, 2000).

31: Moulton is known to be the anonymous subject of the poem "The New Wife and the Old" by John Greenleaf Whittier.

31: *eBay policy*: http://www.businessinsider.com/soul-listing-policy-ebay-2012-7

32: *Plato believed that souls were re-incarnated:* Steward Goetz and Charles Taliaferro, *A Brief History of the Soul* (Malden, MA: Wiley-Blackwell, 2011), 12.

32: *Augustine said that maybe souls preexist:* Ibid., 44–45.

32: *"Now there are some things":* Thornton Wilder, *Our Town* (New York: Harper & Row, 1938), 87–88.

33: *Walking Corpse Syndrome:* G.E. Berrios & R. Luque, "Cotard's Delusion or Syndrome: A Conceptual History," *Comprehensive Psychiatry* 36:3 (May–June 1995): 218–23.

33: Clifford Nass, *The Man Who Lied to His Laptop* (New York: Penguin Books, 2010).

34: Daniel Kahneman, *Thinking Fast and Slow* (New York: Farrar, Straus, and Giroux, 2011), 32.

34: Edmund Hess: cited in Kahneman, *Thinking Fast and Slow,* 32.

34: John McCain: http://blogs.wsj.com/washwire/2007/10/16/mccain-sees-something-in-putins-eyes/

34: *"soulful work" movement:* www.soulfulwork.net

35: *cost to save a soul: The New York Times* (October 9, 1911), section 7.

35: *"I don't deserve a soul":* Douglas Coupland, *The Gum Thief* (New York: Bloomsbury, 2007), 21.

35: *"If a child is born":* Jeffrey Boyd, "One's Self-Concept and Biblical Theology," *Journal of the Evangelical Theological Society* 40:2 (June 1997): 223.

CHAPTER 2: What Is the Soul?

39: *"The LORD God formed man":* Genesis 2:7 KJV.

39: *"What is running your life":* Dallas Willard, *Renovation of the Heart* (Colorado Springs: NavPress, 2012), 199.

41: *"The mind of sinful man":* Romans 8:6 NIV 1984.

43: *"And we were all in the ship":* Acts 27:37 KJV.

43: Leonard Cohen: cited in Parker Palmer, *A Hidden Wholeness* (San Francisco: Jossey-Bass, 2004), 1.

44: *"What does it profit":* Mark 8:36 ESV.

45: Parker Palmer, *A Hidden Wholeness,* 2.

45: *"When we catch sight":* Ibid.

46: *"Treatment of the psyche":* Sigmund Freud, quoted in Jeffrey Boyd, *Reclaiming the Soul* (Cleveland: Pilgrim Press, 1996), 6.

46: *Journal of the American Medical Association:* "The Rising Cost of Modernity," cited in *The New York Times* (December 9, 1992), 8.

46: Martin Seligman, *The Optimistic Child* (New York: Houghton Mifflin, 1996), 25ff.

47: *"I mean, when you sing":* Scott Flaherty: John Colapinto, "Giving Voice," *The New Yorker* (March 4, 2013), 50.

48: *"Though you have not":* 1 Peter 1:8–9 NIV.

48: Horatio Spafford: "It Is Well with My Soul," 1873.

CHAPTER 3: A Soul-Challenged World

52: Ray Romano: Parrott, *You're Stronger Than You Think*, 17.

54: *Parable of the Sower*: Mark 4:1–20.

56: Richard Foster, *Celebration of Discipline* (New York: Harper & Row, 1978), 1.

56: *"As the deer"*: Psalm 42:1, 5, 7.

58: *"My soul is downcast"*: Psalm 42:6, 7.

58: *"I will speak out"*: Job 7:11.

58: *"I will make my dwelling"*: Leviticus 26:11–12 NASB.

58: *"A voice from heaven"*: Matthew 3:17; 12:18, my translation.

59: *Yuppie*: adapted from Matthew 19:16–22; Luke 18:18–23; Mark 10:17–22.

CHAPTER 4: Lost Souls

66: *"You desire truth"*: Psalm 51:6, my translation.

66: *"There are sinful desires"*: 1 Peter 2:11, my translation.

66: *"Bless the LORD"*: Psalm 103:1 KJV, emphasis mine.

67: *"What is the most important"*: Mark 12:28, 30, my translation.

67: *"The divided life"*: Palmer, *A Hidden Wholeness*, 20.

70: *"in my inner being"*: Romans 7:22–23.

70: *"The spirit is willing"*: Matthew 26:41.

CHAPTER 5: Sin and the Soul

71: *Chloé sunglasses study*: Wray Herbert, "Faking It," *Scientific American Mind* (August 23, 2010), https://www.scientificamerican.com/article.cfm?id=faking-it

72: *"Here is a trustworthy"*: 1 Timothy 1:15.

72: John Stott, *Guard the Truth* (Downers Grove, IL: InterVarsity Press), 53.

72: "Neural Consequences of Religious Belief on Self-Referential Processing," *Social Neuroscience* 3:1 (2008): 1–15, doi:10.1080/17470910701469681

73: Jeff Schwartz: personal communication.

73: *"Dear friends"*: 1 Peter 2:11.

73: Dan Ariely, *The Honest Truth about Dishonesty: How We Lie to Everyone—Especially Ourselves* (New York: HarperCollins, 2012).

74: *"the godlessness"*: Romans 1:18.

74: *"Over the course"*: Ariely, *The Honest Truth about Dishonesty*.

74: Mike Adams: "The Dead Grandmother/Exam Syndrome and the Potential Downfall of American Society," *The Connecticut Review* (1990), http://www.psy.gla.ac.uk/~steve/best/grandma.html

76: *"God is merciful"*: Francis Fenelon, *The Royal Way of the Cross* (Cape Cod: Paraclete Press, 1982), 38.

76: *"I remember my affliction"*: Lamentations 3:19–20.

77: *"law of the Lord"*: Psalm 19:7.

CHAPTER 6: It's the Nature of the Soul to Need

82: Hans Walter Wolff, *Anthropology of the Old Testament* (Minneapolis: Augsburg Fortress, 1975), 74.

82: *"We are limited in every way"*: Kent Dunnington, *Addiction and Virtue* (Downers Grove, IL: InterVarsity Press, 2011), 146.

82: *Idolatry is the sin beneath the sin*: Timothy Keller, *Counterfeit Gods* (New York: Riverhead Trade, 2011).

83: *True devotion checklist*: from Gerald May, source unknown by author.

85: *"We are all governed"*: Keller, *Counterfeit Gods*, 141.

85: *"Jacob served seven years"*: Genesis 29:20.

85: *"Today I'm repaying"*: Luke 19:8, my translation.

85: *"My soul yearns"*: Psalm 84:2.

87: Francis Fenelon, *The Royal Way of the Cross*, 1.

CHAPTER 7: The Soul Needs a Keeper

90: *"What do you people mean"*: Ezekiel 18:2–4 NIV 1984.

90: *"You reap what you sow"*: Galatians 6:7, my paraphrase.

91: Adoni-Bezek: Judges 1:5–6.

91: *"Seventy kings"*: Judges 1:7.

92: *"Do not be deceived"*: Galatians 6:7.

92: *"Call this world"*: "John Keats to George and Georgiana Keats," 21 April 1819, in *Letters of John Keats*, vol. 2, ed. H. E. Rollins (Cambridge, MA: Harvard University Press, 1958).

92: *subjects observing angry faces*: M. D. Lieberman, "Putting Feelings into Words," *Psychological Science* 18 (2007): 421–428.

92: *"I am the master of my fate"*: William Ernest Henley, "Invictus: In Memoriam R.T.H.B." (1888).

93: *blessed people are like trees*: Psalm 1:3.

94: *"tell my brother"*: Luke 12:13–21.

94: *"Soul, you have many goods"*: Luke 12:19 NASB.

94: *"You fool"*: Luke 12:20 NASB.

96: *"Both for his own sake"*: Kees Waaijman, "The Soul as Spiritual Core Concept," *Studies in Spirituality* 6 (1996): 7.

96: *"such persons must be cut off"*: Leviticus 18:29.

97: *"Do not be afraid"*: Matthew 10:27–28.

CHAPTER 8: The Soul Needs a Center

99: *"sinkhole syndrome"*: Gordon MacDonald, *Ordering Your Private World* (Nashville: Thomas Nelson, 1984), 15.

100: *"double-minded"*: James 4:8.

100: Pilate: Matthew 27:11–26; Mark 15:1–15; John 18:28–40.

100: *"re-soul"*: 2 Samuel 16:14.

100: Elijah: 1 Kings 19.

101: *"Have mercy on me"*: Psalm 57:1–2.

101: *"their souls grew short"*: Numbers 21:4, translation in Wolff, *Anthropology of the Old Testament*, 17.

101: *"long-souled"*: Waaijman, "Soul as Spiritual Core Concept," 16.

101: King Saul: 1 Samuel 13:5–14.

102: *"Nothing in man"*: Waaijman, "Soul as Spiritual Core Concept," 17.

103: *lift your soul up in pride*: Habakkuk 2:4.

103: *who can live in God's presence*: Psalm 24:2.

103: *"How collapsed"*: Psalm 42:6, translation by Waaijman, "Soul as Spiritual Core Concept," 13.

103: *"Let the morning bring"*: Psalm 143:8, my translation.

104: *"My soul cleaves"*: Psalm 63:8, translation by Waaijman, "Soul as Spiritual Core Concept," 18.

104: Thomas Kelly, quoted in Gordon MacDonald, *Ordering Your Private World* (Nashville: Thomas Nelson, 1984), 120.

104: *"My soul clings"*: Psalm 63:8 NASB.

104: *"My soul thirsts"*: Psalm 42:2.

104: Brother Lawrence, *Practicing the Presence of God* (Springdale, PA: Whitaker House, 1982), 19.

CHAPTER 9: The Soul Needs a Future

107: *"In the day of my trouble"*: Psalm 77:2 NASB, emphasis mine.

107: *"A voice of one"*: Isaiah 40:6–8 WEB.

108: Churchill: William Manchester, *The Last Lion* Vol. 1 (New York: Dell Publishing, 1983), 367.

109: *"[God] has also set"*: Ecclesiastes 3:11.

111: *"The Word became flesh"*: John 1:14.

112: *rescuing the soul*: Psalm 33:19.

112: *escape the sword*: Psalm 34:23.

112: *delivering it from the threshold*: Psalm 142:7.

112: *anything to keep the soul*: translation by Waaijman, "Soul as Spiritual Core Concept" (see Pss. 33:19; 34:23; 142:7).

112: *"In whose hand"*: Job 12:10 KJV, emphasis mine.

112: *"In a little while"*: John 16:16.

112: *"A woman giving birth"*: John 16:21–23.

112: *"In that day"*: John 16:23.

115: *"It is the nature of joy"*: Rudolph Bultmann, quoted in Frederick Dale Bruner, *Gospel of John: A Commentary,* (Grand Rapids: Eerdmans, 2012), John 16:23.

CHAPTER 10: The Soul Needs to Be with God

116: *Indeed, the soul*: Waaijman, "Soul as Spiritual Core Concept," 17.

117: *"heard the sound of the LORD"*: Genesis 3:8.

117: *"the LORD was with Joseph"*: Genesis 39:19–23.

118: *"they will call him Immanuel"*: Matthew 1:23.

118: *"I am the vine"*: John 15:5.

121: Frank Laubach: in letter dated March 9, 1930, in *Letters from a Modern Mystic*, ed. Laubach et al. (New York: Student Volunteer Movement, 1937), 15.

122: *"I have set"*: Psalm 16:8 ESV.

122: *"We take captive"*: 2 Corinthians 10:5.

124: *"From now on"*: 2 Corinthians 5:16.

CHAPTER 11: The Soul Needs Rest

126: *"Come to me"*: Matthew 11:28–30, emphasis mine.

126: Frank Lake: Trevor Hudson and Jerry Haas, *Cycle of Grace* (Nashville: Upper Room, 2012).

127: Cycle of Grace: Ibid.

127: *"You are my son"*: Mark 1:11.

128: *"This is my beloved Son"*: Matthew 17:5 ESV.

129: *"The Son of Man came"*: Matthew 11:19, my translation.

130: Lettie Cowman, *Springs in the Valley* (Grand Rapids: Zondervan, 1939), 41.

130: Roy Baumeister and John Tirney, *Willpower* (New York: Penguin Books, 2011), 24ff.

131: *indicators of soul-fatigue:* Background on this list came from ibid., 245.

132: *"Peace I leave with you"*: John 14:27.

133: *"This is my beloved"*: Matthew 3:17 ESV.

133: *"IF you are"*: Matthew 4:3, 6, my translation.

135: *"Come with me"*: Mark 6:31.

136: *"He makes me lie down"*: Psalm 23:2–3.

138: *"God had finished"*: Genesis 2:2.

138: *"Remember the Sabbath"*: Exodus 20:8–10.

138: Abraham Heschel, *The Sabbath* (New York: Farrar, Straus and Giroux, 2005): 13.

CHAPTER 12: The Soul Needs Freedom

141: *They delight:* Psalm 1:2 TLB.

143: Philip Yancey, *What's So Amazing about Grace?* (Grand Rapids: Zondervan, 1997), 193.

143: *John Calvin's Geneva:* Ibid., 234.

144: *"I am the LORD"*: Exodus 20:2.

146: *"I brought you out"*: Ibid.

147: *"I will always obey"*: Psalm 119:44.

147: *"I will walk about"*: Psalm 119:45.

147: *"whoever looks intently"*: James 1:25.

148: *cure of the soul:* Gregory of Nazianzus, *Oration* 2.16–17 in Phillip Schaff, *Nicene and Post-Nicene Fathers,* Second Series (7).

148: Philip Rieff, *Triumph of the Therapeutic: Uses of Faith after Freud* (Chicago: University of Chicago Press, 1987), 25ff.

148: Barna research group: https://www.barna.org/barna-update/culture/600 -new-years-resolutions-temptations-and-americas-favorite-sins

150: *"I do not understand":* Romans 7:15, 19.

150: *Duke University study:* Charles Duhigg, *The Power of Habit* (New York: Random House, 2012), xv–xvi.

CHAPTER 13: The Soul Needs Blessing

152: Richard Selzer, *Mortal Lessons: Notes on the Art of Surgery* (San Diego: Harcourt Brace, 1996), 16, 46.

154: *"I will eat":* Genesis 27:25, my translation.

154: *"forcefully expresses itself":* Waaijman, "Soul as Spiritual Core Concept," 16.

154: *"Bless me":* Genesis 27:38, my translation.

154: *"The Lord bless you":* Numbers 6:24–26 ESV.

157: *"You shall not oppress":* Exodus 23:9, my translation.

157: *"The soul of Jonathan":* 1 Samuel 18:1–4, my translation.

158: *Celtic Christians on soul friend:* Kenneth Leech, *Soul Friend* (New York: Harper & Row, 1977), p. iii.

158: *"[he] whom my soul loves":* Song of Songs 1:7 ESV.

159: *mirror neurons:* G. Rissolatti, "The Mirror Neuron System," *Annual Review of Neuroscience* 27 (2004): 169–96.

159: *ACC role in response to suffering:* This research summary came from a researcher who wishes to remain anonymous.

160: *"Love your neighbor":* Matthew 19:19.

CHAPTER 14: The Soul Needs Satisfaction

161: *"Why did she look at me . . .?":* Michael Singer: *Untethered Soul* (Oakland, CA: New Harbinger, 2007).

163: *Shechem and Dinah:* Genesis 34.

163: *"His nephesh, his soul . . .":* Genesis 34:3, my translation.

163: *"See, the enemy is puffed up":* Habakkuk 2:4–5a.

163: *"and like death":* Habakkuk 2:5b.

164: *"There is nothing better":* Ecclesiastes 3:22, my translation.

164: *"Because your love is better":* Psalm 63:3, 5, my translation.

164: *"My soul, find rest":* Psalm 62:5.

164: *"whoever wants to save":* Luke 9:24, my translation.

164: *"My heart is not proud":* Psalm 131:1–2, my translation.

165: *Monkey stress and brain research:* For more information about this research, consult the journals *Developmental Neuroscience* 31.4 (2009); *Proceedings of* the National Academy of Science of the United States of America 103.8 (2006) and 107.33 (2010); and *Psychoneuroendocrinology* 32.7 (2007).

167: Kent Dunnington, *Addiction and Virtue*, 141.

168: *"Come, all you who are thirsty"*: Isaiah 55:1 – 2.

CHAPTER 15: The Soul Needs Gratitude

169: *"Do everything without grumbling"*: Philippians 2:14.

170: *"be thankful"*: Colossians 3:15b – 17, my translation.

170: *"give thanks in all"*: 1 Thessalonians 5:18.

170: *"Why, my soul"*: Psalm 42:5.

171: *"Praise the LORD"*: Psalm 103:2 – 5.

171: *"Don't be deceived"*: James 1:16 – 17.

173: *"For although they knew God"*: Romans 1:21.

173: *"forget not"*: Psalm 103:2.

176: *"We can only be said"*: Thornton Wilder, *Our Town*, 1938.

CHAPTER 16: Dark Night of the Soul

182: *"there will come a time"*: St. John of the Cross, *The Dark Night of the Soul*, in *Devotional Classics*, ed. Richard Foster and J. B. Smith (San Francisco: HarperOne, 1993), 33.

182: *"God's love is not content"*: Ibid., 37.

183: *Their problem is that they lack the patience*: Ibid., 35 – 36.

183: *"Break the teeth"*: Psalm 58:6 – 8.

185: Frederick Faber, *Growth in Holiness* (Baltimore: John Murphy, 1854), 120 – 24.

188: *"The one who trusts in me"*: Paraphrase of Matthew 16:28; Mark 9:1; Luke 9:27.

CHAPTER 17: Morning

190: *"[Redeem] the time"*: Ephesians 5:16 KJV.

Acknowledgments

196: *"Let no debt remain outstanding"*: Romans 13:8.